AF804888

A Critical Study of Social Security for Muslim Women under Mohammedan Law

Virendra Mathur

ACKNOWLEDGEMENT

Writing of this page has come in this educational pilgrimage with the blessings of "GOD". I owe my sincere gratitude and heartiest appreciation to all those helping hands and minds that has helped me in the preparation of this manuscript.

I am in extreme drought of words to express my indebtedness and heartfelt thanks to my worthy and revered guide **Prof. (Dr.) Vimlendu Tayal**, Former Vice-Chancellor, University of Bikaner, Bikaner, Principal, N.M. Law P.G. College, Hanumangarh Town (Raj.) for his scholastic guidance, excellent cooperation and persistent motivation during entire period of study.

It is my humble duty to acknowledge, **Dr. M. Tariq**, Sr. Lecturer, N. M. Law P.G. College, Hanumangarh Town, Hanumangarh (Raj.) for moral support and amicable help.

My sincere thanks are also due to all teaching and administrial staff of N.M. Law P.G. College, Hanumangarh for providing necessary facilities during the course of study.

I express my heartiest gratitude to Mr. Dinesh Kumar Sharma, Computer Operator for providing all necessary computer facilities to come out with such an excellent form of thesis..

I am deeply indebted to all the Indian and foreign writers and judges whose writings and decisions have been duly cited in this work and have given me inspiration and light for completing this work. I acknowledge my gratitude to those authors also whose works, though might not have been cited in this thesis, helped me enormously in formulating my views and enriching my thoughts.

In the very last, I thank the almighty "God" once again for giving me strength and perseverance to complete this task.

(Virendra Mathur)

CONTENTS

TABLE OF CASES

A Vs B.:(1896) 21 Bom.71.

A.A. Abdullah Vs. A.B. Mohmuna Begum: AIR (1988) Guj. 143.

Aamin Ali Vs.Mst.Aziz-un-Nisa: AIR 1933 All 329.

Abdul Ghafoor Vs. A.U. Pathumma Beevi : (1989) Cr. J. 1224.

Abdul Qadir Vs. Salima: I.L.R. 8 All 149 (F.B).

Abdul Khadar Vs. Taib Begum: AIR 1957 Mad. 340.

Abdul Latif Mondal Vs. Anuwara Khatun : 2002 (1) e.L.J.186.

Abdul Latif Vs. Niyaz Ahmad: I.L.R.31 (All) 343.

Abdul Rahman Khan Vs. Inyati Bibi : AIR 1931 Oudh 63.

Abdul Rau Khan Vs. Halemon Bibi: (1989) 67 Cr.L.J. 294.

Abdul Razack Vs. Aga Mohammad: (1893) 21 I.A.56.

Abdul Samad Vs. Alimuddin : AIR 1944 (Pat) 174.

Abdul Wahab Khan Vs. Mustaq Ahmed Khan: AIR 1944 A1136.

Abdul Yusuf Vs. Sowramma: AIR 1971 Ker261.

Abdullah Vs. Sharns-ul-Haq : 43 All. 127.

Abdur Rahman Vs. Sheikh Wali Mohammad: AIR 1923 (Pat) 72; 68 C.601.

Abi Dhunisea Bibi Vs. Mohammad Fathiuddin : 44 I.C. 293.

Abid Ali Vs. Mst.Raisa Begum: 1988 (1) Raj.L.R.I04.

Achia Khatoon Vs. Abdul Hai: AIR 1931 Bom 76.

Ahmad Azim Vs. Safi Jan: AIR 1926 Oudh 561.

Ahmed Hussain Vs. Mst. Khodeja : 10 W.R.369.

Aizunnisa Vs. Karimunnisa : (1895)23 Cal.131.

Ajuba Begum Vs. Nazir Ahmed: 1890 W.N. 115.

Ali Baksh Vs. Allahbad Khan: 32 All 557: I.L.R. 32 All 551.

Ali Bhunimsa Bibi Vs. Mohd. Fathia Uddin: 1918 (41) Mad.1026.

Ali Mohammad Khan Vs. Azizullah Khan: 1883 W.N. 204.

Ali Vs. Safaria : (1988) 2 K.L.T. 94.

Allah Diwaya Vs. Kammon Mai: PLD 1957 (W.P.) Lah.651.

Ameer Ammal Vs. Sankaranarayanan : (1904) All. L.J. 394.

Amir Hasan Vs. Mohd. Nasir Hasan: AIR 1932 All 345.

Anis Begam Vs. Mohd. Istefa: (1933) 55 All 743.

Arab Ahmadia Vs. Arab Bail: AIR 1988 (Guj.) 141.

Asia Khatun Vs. Amarendra Nath Babu : AIR 1940 Cal. 578.

Asma Bibi Vs. Abdul Jamal: I.L.R (All) I.C. (44) 167: 5.

Atiqa Begum Vs. Mohd. Ibrahim: AIR 1916 PC 250 & 36 IC

Aziza Khan Vs. Amir Hussain: (2000) Cr. L.J. 2582

Azizullah Khan Vs. Ajmed Ali Mohammad: 1885 W.N. 54.

B.M. Mondal Vs. D.R. Bibi : AIR 1971 Cal. 162.

Babe Vs. Janee: 2 N.W.P. 319.

Babee Bachun Vs. Hamid Hussain: (1871) 14 M.I.A. 37.

Baddruddin Vs. Aisha Begum: 1957 All L.J. 300.

Bai Fatrna Vs. Ali Mohammed Aiyeb : (1912) 37 Bom. 280.

Bai Tahira Vs. Ali Hussain Fissalli Clothia : 1979 Cr. L.J. 151.

Bashir Ali Vs. Hafiz Nazir : 4 I.C, 462.

Beeiu Bee Vs. Syed Moorthuja : AIR 1920 Mad. 666.

Bibi Jambi Vs. Abbaj All. AIR 1941 Nag. 167.

Bibi Kabra Vs. Jainandan Prasad: AIR 1955 (Pat) 270.

Bibi Makbul-un-Nissa Vs. Bibi Umat-un-Nisa : AIR 1923 Pat.153.

Bindeshri Pershad Vs. Afzal Khan: AIR 1921 All 242.

Cap. Ramesh Chandra Kaushal Vs. Mrs. Veena Kaushaland, 1979 Cr. J.J.3.

Ch.Shakar S Dass Vs. Mahbub Jan: AIR 1942 Peshwar 92.

Chuni Bibi Vs. Shams-un-Nissa Bibi: (1894) All 19: (1894) 7 All 79.

Danial Latif Vs. Union of India : (2001) 7 SCC 740.

E V Kuhirnariam Vs. O.Marnmu AIR 1985 (Ker) 239.

Eidan Vs Mazhar Hussain' LL.R.I (AII) 483.

Ekram Hussain vs. AlI Hussain: 17 Pat L.J. 423.

Fatima Vs. Sader-ud -din : 1865 (2) B.H.C.R. 291.

Fazlumbi V s. Khader Vali : AI R 1980 SC 1730 : 19804 SCC 125 .

Fazlur Rahman Vs. Aisha: 19291.L.R. 8 (Pat) 690.

Ful Chand Vs. Nazab Ali Choudhary: (1909) AIR 36 Cal 185:

Ghana Kanta Mohania Vs. Gereli: (1904) 32 Cal 479,

Ghisuddin Babu Khan Vs. Commissioner of Income Tax: A.P. III, Hyd. 1985

Hadi Ali Vs. Akbar Ali: 40 All 262.

Hafijabi Vs. Suleman Darwajkar: AIR 1996 (Bom) 80.

Haji Mokshed Mandai Vs. Del Rushon Bibi : AIR 1971 (62) Cal. 162.

Hamidoola Vs. Faizunnisa : (1812) 8 Ca1.327.

Hamiduca Bibi Vs. Zaheer Shaikh: 17 Cal. 670.

Hamira Bibi Vs. Zubaida Bibi : LLR. 38 All 58.

Hannefa Vs. Pathummal : 1972 KLT 512.

Haroon Rashid Vs. Raqueeba Khatoon: (1997) I B.L.J.R. 93.

Hasenura Begum Vs. Fazar Ali: (2001) 3 Gau Law Reports 576.

Hazraru Vs. Rahman: (1989) CLLJ. 1519.

Hussan Vs. Rahim Khan: AIR 1954 Mys. 24.

Hussein Khan Vs. Ghulab Khatoon : I.L.R. 35 Bom.386.

Hyder Khan Vis. Mehr-un-Nisa: 1993 Cr.L.J. 236.

In Re Din Muhammad: (1882) 5 All 226. 231.

Iqbal Ahmad Khan Vs. State of U.P. :1960 Cr. L.J. (NOC) 80 (All).

Jahurdan Vs. Sakina Bibi : AIR 1934 Cal. 210 : 149L.C. 1150.

Jai-ud-din Ahmed Vs. Anwara Begum: 1981 (I) G.L.R. 358.

Jarnait Ali Saheb Vs. Mir.Mohammad: (1916) Panjab Record.

Julekha Vs. M.Fazal : 2000 (I) Vidhi Bhaswar 123 M.P.

Jyani Begum Vs. Umrav Begum: 1908 1.L.R. 32 (Bom) 612.

K.e.Moyin Vs. Nafeesa: AIR 1973 Ker.176.

Kaka Vs. Hassan Banu : 1998 (2) D.M.C. 85.

Kallo Vs. Mst. Imaman : AIR 1949 All 445.

Kamar-un-Nissa Bibi Vs. Hussaini Bibi : (1881) 3AIl 266 (PC).

Kamlakshi Vs. Sankaran: AIR 1979 Ker. 117.

Kaniz Fatima Vs. Ram Nandan Dhar Dube : AIR 1923 All 331.

Kapoor Chand Vs. Kidar Nissa: AIR 1953 SC 413.

Karim Abdul Rehman Vs. Shehnaz Karim: :2000 (3) M.LJ. 555.

Khatun Vs. Amarendra Nath Basu : AIR 1940 Cal. 578.

Khoo Hooi Leong Vs. Khoo Hean Kwel : (1926) A.C. 529.

Khurshid Khan Amin Khan Vs. Husna Bano: 1976 Cr. LJ. 1584.

Khyrunneesa Vs. Alair : 200 I (I) K.L.J. 46.

Koushar Ali Laskar Vs. Moslema Bibi : 2000 (2) Cr. J. 134.

Kulsambi Vs. Bilankhan: AIR 1929 (Nag) 121: 1171.C.220

Kunhi Moyin Vs. Pathumma Gopalan Numbiyar: (1976) K.L.T. 87.

Mahboban Bibi Vs. Moh. Ammer-ud-din : 1929 AIR (Pat) 207.

Mahboob Ali Khalid Vs. Abdul Reed Zeeshan: (1999) Cr. L.J. 3822.

Mainabibi Vs. Choudhry Vakil Ahmad: AIR 1925 (P.C.) 63.

Majid Vian Vs. Bibi Saheb : I.L.R. 40 Bom.34.

Majidmian Baxumian Vs. Bibi Sahabijan: I.L.R. 40 Born 34.

Majitha Beevi Vs. Yakoob: 1999 (I) K.L.T. 796.

Makbul-un-Nissa Vs. Umatumnisa: AIR 1923 Pat.33 ;

Marina Jalos Vs. Nuruddin Jatoi : P.L.D. 1967 (SC) 580.

Masltan Sahib Vs. Assam Bibi : I.L.R. 23 (Mad.) 371 [FB].

Md. Zabai Vs. Bibi Sahidan: AIR 1942 (Pat) 210

Mia Khan Vs. Bibi Jan: 5 Beng. L.R. 500.

Mir Abdul Rehman Vs. Nurjahan Nur Bibi: (2000) Cr.L.J. 1949.

Mir Vahedali Kadumiya Vs. Rashid Beg Kadumiya : AIR 1951 Bom.22.

Modhi Vs. Kallendar: AIR 1927 PC 15.

Mohammad Ali Mohammad Khan Vs. Mst.Bismillah Begum: AIR 1930 P.C.255.

Mohammad Jahir Vs. Nazral Fatima: I.L.R. 1995 Kant 2259; 1995 Cr.L.J. 3822.

Mohammad Shahabuddin Vs. Mst.Umator Rasool: AIR 1960 (Pat.) 511.

Mohammad Subhanallah Vs. Saghirunnisa: 1911 (41) All 562.

Mohammad Vs. Saira Bai : 1976 K.L.T. 711.

Mohammad Yameed Vs. State of U.P. : (1992) Cr.L.J. 1804.

Mohd. Ahmad Khan Vs. Shah Bano Begum: AIR 1985 SC 945: (1985) 2 SCC 556.

Mohd. Ibrahim Vs. Ma Ma : 1939 (Rang) 28.

Mohd. Karimullah Vs. Arnarn Begum: I.I.R 17 All 93.

Mohd. Shahabuddin Vs. Mst.Umator Paroo : AIR 1960511 ; I.L.R. 38 (Pat) 624.

Mohd. Shamsuddin Vs. Noor Jahan: AIR 1955 (Hyd) 144.

Mohd. Umar Khan Vs. Gulshan Begum: 1992 Cr. L.J.899.

Mohd. Yunus Vs. Bibi Phankani Tasrum Nisa.: 1987 (2) Crimes 241.

Mohd. Zabain Vs. Mst.Bibi Sahidan: 1942 AIR (Pat) 217.

Mohd. Zobair Vs. Bibi Sahidan: AIR 1942 (Pat) 210;

Munshi Buz-ul-Raheem Vs. Lateefa-un-Nissa: (1861) 8 M.I.A.379.

Mst Nawab Begum Vs. Hussain Ali Khan: AIR 1937 Lah. 589.

Mst. Amina Bibi Vs. Ibrahim: AIR 1929 Oudh 520.

Mst. Mainunnav. Vs. Sharafatillah : AIR 1931 (All) 403: 29 A L.J. 197.

Mst.Bibi Makbul Unnisa Vs. Mst. Bibi Umatunnisa : AIR 1923 (Pat) 33.

Mst.Fahiman Vs. Bulaq: AIR 1935 Oudh 68.

Mst.Ghulam Kubra Vs. Mohammad Shaft: AIR (1940) Peshawar 2.

Mst. Zainaba Vs. Abdul Rahman: AIR (1945) Peshawar 5 I.

Mst.Haliman Vs. Mohd. Monir: AIR 1971 Pat.385.

Mst.Jaddo Begum Vs. Nawab Sharaf Begum: AIR 1921 Oudh 194.

Mst.Kumur-ul-Nissa Begum Vs. Mahomed Hussain: (1866) I Agra 266.

Mst.Mahtabunnisa Vs. Rifaqatullah: AIR 1925 (All) 474: 85 i.c. 459.

Mst.Nasiban Bi Vs. Mst.lqbal Begum: AIR 1935 Lah. 816.

Mst.Zohra Khatoon Vs. Md.lbrahim: AIR 1981 SC 1243.

Muzaffar Ali Vs. Parbati : I.L.R. 29 All 640 :

Mysore State E. Board Vs. Bangalor W.e.& S. Mills: AIR 1963 SC 1128.

Nabijan Vs. Sahifan: AIR 1923 Pat. 153.

Naksetan Bibi Vs. Habibar Rahaman : 50 e.W.N. 689.

Nansur Vs. Azizul : (1928) 3 Luck 603.

Naseem Vs.State of U.P.: 1998 All L.J. 2270.

Nasir-ud-Din Shah Vs. Amatul Mughni: 1948 (Lah) 135 (FB).

Nawab Sadiq Ali Khan Vs. Jai Kishori : (1928) 30 Bom. L.R.1346.

Nizar Vs. Hyrunneessa: 1999 (1) K.L.T. 709.

Noor Sabha Khatoon Vs. Md. Qasim: (1997) Cr. L.J. 3972.

Nurjahan Bibi Vs. Mohd. Kazim Ali: AIR 1977 Cal 90.

Nurunnissa Khanam Vs. Khaja Mohd. Sakru: I.L.R. (1920)47 Ca1537.

Patnam Vahedullah Khan Vs. Ashia Khatoon : (2000) Cr. L.J. 2124.

Qayyum Khan Vs. Moorunisa: 1978 Cr. L.J.1476.

Rabia Khatoon Vs. Mukhtar Ahmed: 1966 AIR (All) 548: 1966 All. L.J.182

Rafiq Vis. Farida Bi : 2000 (2) M.P.W.N. 77 M.P.

Rahema Khatoon Vs. Iqtidar-ud-din : AIR 1943 (All) 184.

Ram Lal Mookerjee Vs. Hasan Chandra Dhar: 3 Beng L.R. 130.

Ram Prasad Singh Vs. Mst.Bibi Khoda: AIR 1944 (Pat) 163.

Ramzaan Vs. Smt. Salma: (1997) Cr. L.J. (Raj.) 324.

Rashid-un-Nissa Vs. Ata Rasool : 1958 AIR (All) 67.

Rehana Khatoon Vs. Iqtidaruddin: AIR 1943 (All) 184 P. 187.

Rizwana Begum Vs. Motiullah: (1989) Cr. L.J. (NOC) 156.

Rukia Khatun Vs. Abdul Khalik Laskar: 1981 (I) G.L.R. 375.

Rukshana Parveen Vs. S.K. Mohammad: 1977 Cr. L.J. 1041.

Saburunnisa Vs. Sabdu Shaikh: AIR 1934 (Cal) 693.

Sarb Krishan Vs. Mst.Fatima : 1937 AIR (Lah) 859.

Sarwari Vs. Shaf. Mohammad: (1957) J All 255.

Shaikh Md. Zubair Vs. Bibi Sahidan : AIR 1942 (Pat) 2 J O.

Shaikh Mohammad Zubair Vs. Mst. Bibi Sahidan : AIR 1942 (Pat) 210 : 1971.C. 241

Shaikh Mohd. Zubair Vs. Bibi Suhidan : AIR 1942 (Pat) 210.

Shaikh Salima Vs. Shaikh Mohd.: AIR 1961 All 428.

Shakila Parveen Vs. Haider Ali: (2000) 1 CLJ 608.

Shamim Ara Vs. State of U.P.: 2002 (7) SCC 518.

Shazada Qauram Vs. Fakher Jung : AIR 1953 (Hyd) -134.

Sheikh Abdur Rahman Vs. Saikh Wah Mohammad: AIR 1923 Pat. 72.

Sheikh Mohammad Rowther Vs. Aiyesa Bibi: 1938 AIR (Mad) 107.

Sheikh Mohd. Vs. Bibi : AIR 1938 (Mad.) 107.

Shohrat Singh Vs. Jafri Bibi : 24 I.C. 499 P.C.

Smt. Hamidan Vs. Md. Rafiq: (1994) Cr.L.J 348.

Smt.Jaitunbi Mubarak Shaikh Vs. Mubarak Fakruddin Shaikh: (1999) Cr.L.J.3846.

Srinivasn Iyyer Vs. Saraswati : AIR 1952 Mad. 193.

Sughra Bibi Vs. Gaya Prasad: AIR 1930 All 580.

Sughra Begum Vs. Mohd. Mir : I.L.R. 43 All. 341.

Syed Ahmad Vs. Banyadi : 26 P.K. 429.

Syed Ahmed Khan Vs. Smt. Imrat Jahan Begum: 1982 AIR (All) 1555.

Syed Fazal P.T Vs. Union of India: AIR 1993 Ker.308.

Syed Hamid Khan Vs. Ms Uammibai : 1978 I.L.R. (MP) 595.

Syed Sabir Hussain Vs. Farzand Hussain: 1937 (65) I.A.119, 127 Fat Law 669.

T. N. WakfBoard Vs. Syed Fatima Nachi : AIR 1998 SC 2423.

Tufail Ahmad Vs. Jamila Khatun: 1962 All L.J. 971.

Umar Hayat Khan Vs. Mahabubunnisa: 1976 Cr. L.J. 395.

Usrnan Khan Bahamani Vs. Fathim-un-Nisa Begum: AIR 1990 (A.P.) 225.

Wajid Ali Vs. Jaffar Hussain: AIR Oudh 34.

Yunus Vs. Bibi Phenkani Tabnun Nisa: (1987) 2 Crimes 241.

Zaib-un-Nisa Vs. Nazim Hasan: AIR 1962 All 197: 1961 All L.J. 892.

Zobair Ahmed Vs. Jain and an Prasad Singh: AIR 1960 (Pat) 147.

Zohra Khatoon Vs. Mohd. Ibrahim: AIR 1981 SC 1243.

CHAPTER-I

CHAPTER - I
Introduction

The issue of women in Islam is topic of great misunderstanding and distortion due partly to a lack of understanding, but also partly due to misbehavior of some Muslims which has been taken to represent the teachings of Islam. We speak here about what Islam teaches, and that is that standard according to which Muslims are to be judged. As such, my basis and source is the Quran--the words of Allah, and the sayings of the Prophet, his deeds and his confirmation. Islamic laws are derived from these sources. To facilitate our discussion we can discuss the position of women from a spiritual, economic, social, and political standpoint.

The best way to judge a nation's progress is to find out the status of women there. The position of women in a society is the true index of its cultural and spiritual attainments. Since the origin of society, women have formed an integral part of social structure. Her role in the various walks of life has contributed to the evolution of values which have counted for what may be described, all round progress. Her status is the measuring rod in assessing the standard of culture of any age. A major index of progress of any society is the position of its women vis-a-vis men. The more balanced the opportunity structure for men and women, the larger the role women have in society, such as that of India. Unfortunately. their contribution is not recognised and they ever remain at disadvantaged position. They are excluded from societal resources, due to lack of education technical knowledge and lack of information. The vast majority of women are victims of complication of feudal and religious fundamentalists. The women are still being treated as commodity and as a result more atrocities on women arc on the rise. Due to gender bias, women are deprived from gender justice. This is true fact about women all over the world without any distinction on the basis of race, class, region, society or nation thus Indian women are no exception. If anybody wants to study the status of women in any society one must study the complexity of roles which women perform in society in the socio-economic, cultural, religious and political fields. It is also important to find out such factors as how they face the problems and situations that arc connected with their sex roles from birth to death and how they adjust themselves to these role situations. This role of women has differed from society to society and from time to time.

The position of women in Muslim society is always a subject for discussion in general. It is usually said that the Islam is an enemy of women for it degrades her and lowers her status holding her intellectually deficient and assigning her a position very much akin to that of animals. She is reduced to not more than a mere means of sensual gratification for man and a machine for the propagation of the human species: which is sufficient to show how subservient to man she is in the sight of the Islam, with the result that man dominates her and enjoys an all round superiority over her. It is a popular fallacy that a Muslim male enjoys an unbridled authority over Muslim female, it begins more specifically after her marriage that she does not have a respectable life to spend and there is no provision for her social security whether it is a issue of Mahr, Divorce, or Maintenance, she always finds herself in the ocean of deep sorrow and loneliness.

The women's rights are human rights and this conclusion is one side of picture relating to the Islam, like other religions of the world Islam too, recognise women's rights as integral and consider them important to the effective functioning of the society. The Islam works on the foundation that the biological and psychological differences between the men and women do exist, it keeps those differences as they are and it employs those differences for determining their place and responsibilities in the social system, the Islam has granted the woman vast social and economic rights, elevated her status and provided such moral and legal safe guards in its system for the protection of her rights and status that can not be found in any other social system.

The Holy book Quran addresses its followers as believers only, not as men and women of any particular class or community of any particular religion. The Sura-al-Nisa[1] is the Holy verse, which speaks of the equality between men and women as "O Mankind! Your (Rabb), who created you from a single person created, of like nature. (its) mate, and from them twin scattered countless men and women: Ye demand your mutual (rights) and (show Taqwa for) the wombs (that bore you) for God ever watches over you."

The Islamic Law does not recognise and distinction between them in so far as protection of life and property, honour and reputation is concerned. But the mere mention of this fact does not fully convey the idea of how highly Islam has honoured woman and elevated her status in the society. The history of human civilisation bears evidence that woman was regarded as an embodiment of depravity, shame and sin in the world. The birth of a daughter so embarrassed a father that he could not raise his head for shame. The in-law relations were looked upon as mean and disgraceful, for this reason, the custom of disposing of daughters by killing them had become common among many nations.

Besides the illiterate, ignorant people, the learned scholars and religious leaders also disputed for generations; the question whether woman was a human being, and whether the Almighty God had granted her a soul. The Islam had indeed changed the mentalities of both the man and the woman. The concept of giving the woman her rights and a place of honour in society has in fact been created in man's mind by the Islam. The slogans of women's rights. women's education and women's emancipation that one so often hears these days are in fact an echo of the revolutionary call of the Holy Prophet Mohammad who changed man's ways of thinking for all times to come. It was the Prophet Mohammad of the Islam, who first taught the world that woman is as much a human being as man and the God does not distinguish between man and woman:[2]

"The men shall have their due share according to what they have earned and the women according to what they have earned."

The high places of honour and distinction that man can attain by virtue of his faith and righteous deeds are also attainable by woman. If a man can become Ibrahirn-bin-Adham, nothing can prevent a woman from becoming Rabi'ah Basri.

"Their Lord answered their prayer [and said]: 1 never let go to waste the labour of anyone that works among you. whether male or female, for in my sight all of you are alike."

"And those who do good works, whether men or women, provided that they are Believers, will enter into Paradise and they will not be deprived in the least of their right/it rewards ".

The Holy Prophet Mohammad warned the man and infused the feeling in the woman that she had the same rights up on him as he had upon her[3]

"Wives have the same rights as the husbands have on them in accordance with the well-known principles."

The Prophet Mohammad further raised the woman from disgrace and shame to the place of honour and dignity. He told the father that the birth of daughter did not bring him any shame: bringing her up and educating her was rather a means of his salvation. It was the Prophet Mohammad who pointed out her own legal rights for the protection of which she could go to law. The woman had found such a merciful sympathetic and strong supporter of their rights in the person of the Prophet Mohammad that they would freely approach him with all sorts of complaints against bad treatment of their husbands. The men, on the contrary, were cautious and careful not to give their wives and chance to complaint against them to the Holy Prophet Mohammad. Abdullah-binUmar has reported that during the lifetime of the Prophet Mohammad the companions treated their wives most politely for fear that a commandment concerning them might be sent down, and not until he had passed away they began talking with them freely. According to the tradition contained in the collection by Ibn-i-Majah, the Holy Prophet Mohammad had forbidden maltreatment of women. Once Hazrat Umar complained that the women had grown insolent and sought permission to have resort to beating to set those rights. The Prophet Mohammad granted the permission and the same day seventy women were beaten in their houses by the husbands who had long been awaiting such permission. The next day all the women thronged the Holy Prophet's house with bitter complaints. The Prophet Mohammad called the people together and addressed them :

"Today severely women have visited to the Holy Prophet Mohammad's house complaining against the harsh treatment oftheir husbands'. The men who have misbehaved in that manner are certainly not the best among you. "

The effect of this moral and legal reform was that the woman attained such a high status in the Islamic society that it has no precedent in the in history. The Muslim women correct indeed has the right to attain the highest place of honour and advancement materially, intellectually and spiritually, both in religious and mundane spheres open to the Muslim male. Her sex does not stand in her way at any stage. The world of today, even in this 20th century, falls for short of this Islamic standard. Human intellectual development has not so far touched the mark set by the Islam. The Holy book has not only given her right to equal status hut also right to education and equal rights to contract, to enterprise, to earn, and posses independently. Almost 14 centuries ago Prophet Mohammad declared that the pursuit of knowledge is incumbent on every Muslim male and female. Thus, it reveals from the study of the Islam that a woman is equal to may bearing personal and common responsibilities and in receiving rewards for her achievements and deeds she is acknowledged as an independent personality in possession of human qualities and worthy of spiritual aspirations. Her human nature is neither inferior nor deviant to that of man. Both are members of one another's society God says:

"And their Lord has accepted [their prayers] and answered them [saving]......................Never will I cause to be lost the work of any of you, be he male orfemale : you are members of one another."

So in the Islamic Law the legal, moral and social status of woman is not affected in any way. As a religion Islam on the one hand, safeguards all her rights by law on the other hand, instructs society to render her a kind and fair treatment, Islam creates such an environment that whatever position woman assumes, she holds it, with all dignity and honour. As long as such an encouragement prevails, no change can be even occur in her honour and dignity. There are three prominent position of woman at home a daughter, a wife and a mother. Islam bestow great rank and position on her in all three roles. No one can pull her back from this high position.

The Islam assigns the highest rank, after Almighty God, His Prophet Mohammad & Mother. The Islam instructs man to give just and fair treatment to both father and mother and commands him for their obedience because both of them confer benevolence on him. But, in the Quran and Hadith, reference to the great benevolence of mother occurs more evidently and prominently. The Quran says:

And we have enjoined on man (to be good) to his parents: in travail upon travail.

Did his mother bear him,

And in years twain

Was his weaning (hear the command) Show gratitude to Me and to your parents:

To Me is (your final) goal.

At another place Allah Almighty says:

We have enjoined on man Kindness to his parents:

In pain did his mother Bear him, and in pain

Did she give him birth

The carrying of the (child)

To his weaning is (a period of) thirty months[4]

To bear the burden of pregnancy for nine long months, to give birth to a child after a great struggle of life and death and to feed her child out of her own blood and to lead a life of full care and strict precaution in all these stages is not at all an easy task. Father does not undertake all these hardships and does not bear all this pain. Therefore, the benevolence and favours of mother on man are more than those of the father. There are several Hadiths which draw the attention towards rendering great service and obedience to mother and behave respectfully with her. Some of its precepts are: -

1. The Holy Prophet Mohammad instructed man to give fair and just treatment to both father and mother. But the Prophet stressed the fair treatment more to mother. The Prophet Mohammad said: 'I

enjoin man about his mother, I enjoin man about his mother, I enjoin man about his mother. I enjoin man about his mother.[5]

2. A separate instruction is also given forbidding disobedience to mother which is condemned as an unlawful act. The Prophet Mohammad said: Allah has forbidden you to be undutiful to your mothers, to withhold (what you should give) or demand (what you do not deserve), and to bury your daughters alive.[6] The Prophet Mohammad mentioned sins and said that when his Ummah perpetrates these sins, great difficulties and torment will fall upon them.

3. The just and fair treatment to mother is regarded as a means of atonement for one's sins and the attainment of Paradise.

4. Service to mother is superior to the service to father. It is next only to the mother that the position of any other person can be determined. Your mother, The man asked: who (deserves) the next? The Prophet Mohammad replied: Your mother, the man enquired for the third time that who deserves the next? The Prophet Mohammad made the same answer: Your mother, When the man repeated the same question for the fourth time. The Prophet Mohammad said, Your father. There are different Traditions on the question whether the polite behaviour with mother should be double or triple? Immam Tahawi says that in this connection those Traditions are more authentic in which it is said that a man should offer kind and mild treatment to mother three times more than what he should offer to his father. Imam Ahmad says that father should be obeyed, but as far as

the fair treatment is concerned, out of the four parts, three belong to mother.

The Islam does not stress the legal rights of mother and father alone but also prescribes a kind and decent treatment to them. The Islam holds that the legal rights of parents should be observed heartily and with love and devotion and should not he regarded as burden. It also unfolds the fact that apart from the legal rights, one should give as noble and humble treatment to parents as possible and in this treatment again, mother deserves more affectionate treatment. Mother should be offered better behaviour than what is offered to father.

For daughters, the teachings of Islam are very crystal clear and they are given very generous treatment. Before the proclamation of the prophet-hood of the Prophet Mohammad parents were much proud of their sons and they were supposed to be their great asset, because they gave more strength to their tribe and they and they were assistants in their great exertion in the field of finance. But daughters were considered to be burden on them and they were supposed to be cause of ignominy or disgrace. The Quran, portrays a very graphic picture of the feelings of a parent on the birth of his daughter at that time in its own eloquent style:

When news is brought to one of them of the Birth of a female (child) his face

Darkness, and he is filled

With inward grief!

With shame does he hid

Himself from his people,

because of the bad news

He has had. Shall he retain it

On (sufferance and) contempt or bury it In the dust.

One of the results of these obnoxious feelings for daughter was that some tribes used to bury their daughters alive. The Quran vehemently criticised the murdering of children and regarded it a capital offence and put an end to this abhorrent practice once and for all. The Quran says that on the last day, one would have to answer for the hard-heartedness to God. The Quran says:

When the female (infant) Buried alive, is Questioned-

For what crime

She was killed.

The Islam inculcated totally different feelings for girls in place of their barbarous and brutal feelings. There is exhortation in the Islam for the proper nourishment and sustenance of daughters. It is regarded as a good deed and a means for the attainment of Heaven. Hazrat Aisha relates that Prophet Mohammad said:

Whoever is in charge of (put to test by)

Three daughters and treats them generously,

Then they will act as a shield for him

From the (Hell) Fire.

In Traditions, the upbringing and nourishment of two or three daughters or sisters or even one daughter or sister is referred to as a means for entering Heave. From this the reward or requital to the person who brings up more than three daughters or sisters can be well realised. Hazrat Itba-bin-Aamir relates that Prophet Mohammad said:

"Whoever has three daughters, and bears with the miseries in their connections, feeds and clothes them with the earnings of his labour, they will become a curtain on the fire of hell for him."

It is stated in Hadith that with the good nourishment of daughters, they should also be given good education and training and should also select a good match for the marriage and should continue fair and just treatment with them.

Generally more love and affection is showered on sons in feeding, clothing, education & training and in every respect more preference is accorded to them. This is total injustice and oppression. In Hadith such a treatment is forbidden and condemned. In all these Hadith on the proper nourishment, education training, arrangement or marriage and equal treatment to daughters or sisters, glad tidings is given for liberation from Hell and the attainment of Heaven. One who does not have faith in God and the eternal day and one who gives all importance to the present world alone does not realise the significance of these Traditions. But the very goal of the believer (Momin) is success on the Judgment Day.

There is all what he wishes in this goodness for a believer. Such a teaching for a fair and just treatment of girls is an example which is found. According to Islamic Law, if the child does not own any position and does not have any proper means for living, his maintenance is obligatory on his father. In accordance with this rule, the maintenance or allowances for daughters is obligatory on his father till her marriage and in the absence of his father, it is necessary for her nearest relative to ensure her maintenance.

After marriage, the responsibility or her maintenance shifts to her husband and on the death of her husband or in case of divorce and if the woman is not self-sufficient in financial matters, the responsibility goes to her children or in case she has no children, the responsibility for her maintenance falls on her nearest relative. This is a legal right and in the Tradition its importance is well emphasised.

As far as her role as a wife is concerned she is not a play thing for husband and he does not enjoy unbridle powers over her. In the Islam woman possess an independent entity of her own. Because of Nikah, neither her responsibilities get dissolved in the personality of her husband nor does she become his subject or servant. When she holds some new responsibilities after marriage, she becomes the owner of some new rights at the same time. Her rights can not be taken away. There is some legal and moral basis, Islam provides for this relationship:

1. The relation of husband and wife is, infect, the relation of love, affection, and intimacy as described in the Holy Quran.[7]
   And among his signs
   As this, that he created
   F or you mates from among.
   Yourselves, that ye may
   Dwell in tranquillity with them
   And he has put love

And mercy between your [hearts]
Verily in that are signs
For those who reflect.

2. There is always a head of every minor in the institution. In Islam, man obtains the position of a head of the family for several reasons, but it does not mean that man has acquired unlimited and whole and sole authority on his wife. Woman, while accepting the superiority of man in domestic life, gains, and enjoys all rights of maintenance residence alimony and education and training and several other rights. If a man falls short of performing all these rights of woman, she can secure them through law for her social security.
3. The Islam exhorts man not only to discharge the legal rights of his wife but to behave with her decently and justly. Nice treatment with wife is required in every condition. Allah says in Almighty the Quran:[8]

On the contrary I ive with them,
On a footing of kindness and equity,
If ye take a dislike to them.
It may be that ye dislike.
A thing, and Good brings about,
Through it a great deal of good.

Hence, the man whose behaviour with his wife is just and fair is regarded as the best man.

It is clear from the above study that what type of relationship Islam wants to promote between husband and wife. If such a type of relationship exists between them, both of them will be assistant and well wisher of each other, their life will be pleasant, and ideal and all the unpleasant problems of rights and demand which cause disturbance and destroy the domestic life would never occur in their life. In this way, in the family system of Islam, the legal right of women is secured. On she holds not only a respectable status in society but there exists provision for social security.

"The scholar has made her sincere effort analyse the position of Muslim women while keeping in view about the social security of Muslim women within the pursuit of Islam for which the study is strictly adhered to three major aspects of Muslim women's security viz. Mahr, Maintenance and Inheritance."

Under Islamic Law a woman has absolute rights of getting Mahr, and Maintenance and her Share is also secured according to Inheritance Law. To assess and determine the actual position of Muslim women and how much she is secured in Islamic Law, this study has been done. With the object to bring out the actual social condition and what are the Quranic ordains exist with regard to women's security more specifically for Mahr, Maintenance and Inheritance. This is the study to analyse the original Islamic view point and judicial attitude on the question of security for Muslim women, keeping in view the need of time and demand of circumstances. In the recent past, it has been observed that the courts have delivered their verdict which are not (with due regard to the court) in consonance with the spirit of Islamic Law. Keeping the above observation in view the study of important judgements in the matters of Marriage, Mahr, Maintenance and Divorce, which are related to social security of Muslim women, has been done.

In addition, it is submitted that law and religion in Islam are so connected together that they cannot easily be separated to each other. The two streams of Shariah and Fiqh flow in a single channel. The Shariah embraces both law and religion, sometimes pulling each other in the opposite direction. The needs of present changing theme demand a new out look of the Islamic Law which is not revealed yet or it has been wrongly interpreted. Fyzee says:[9]

"Laws are like metals in the crucible of time and circumstances: they melt, they gradually solidify into different shapes, they remit and assume diverse forms The process of evolution conterminous with human society. Nothing is static except that which is dead and lifeless Law can never be static."

Thus, the Shariah[10] Whether in its original and some modified from still represents the family law of nearly 425 Million Muslims and still represents the basic law throughout most of the Arabian Peninsula. Thirdly, that it represents a coherent, well documented and independent system of law which will amply repay comparative study. Fourthly, that it still holds the key to the future, for their attitude to this law; the future development of the Muslim countries must largely depend.

As the study reveals that the far reaching and human reforms have been brought about by the Holy Prophet Mohammad and Islam. Though, the Islam attaches great value to education and prescribes it as the duty of a woman as well as that of a man to acquire knowledge.

But in actual practice of Muslim community especially their women facing problem, due to lack of education and knowledge. According to Ilse Lichtenstadter[11]

"fundamentally it (Islam) has always considered learning at least a useful accessory to being a good Muslim ".

The Islam thinks that education is a necessary condition which keeps women to develop their facilities. In the words of Mohammed Qutb[12] acquisition of knowledge in fact is as a great duty of women as of a man, for Islam wanted the woman folk to develop their rational faculties along with physical ones and thus ascend to higher planes of spiritual existence.

The Prophet Mohammed preached his followers "knowledge enables its possessor to distinguish what is forbidden from what is not, it lights the way to heaven, it is our friend in the desert, our society in solitude, our companion with benefit of friends, it guides us to happiness. So in the life of people education has been given importance by Islam. Though Prophet Mohammed favoured women's education, in actual practice the injunctions of the Quran in this respect or completely ignored in result. The Muslim community has misinterpreted many principles of Islam specially provisions which are related for women in connection with their relations with men, because of their negligence towards education. As a result which for the upliftment of women socially and economically, education is a need of time so that they can enjoy then rights given to them. The knowledge of their rights can only secure them. Once they have knowledge of rights then only they would be able to achieve them successfully. A detailed study relating to Marriage, Dower, Divorce, Maintenance and Inheritance of this research will amply testify as to the improvements effected by I slam, particularly the way in which it has elevated the position of women by providing them social security.

The Islamic Law is basically based on the Quran and the Hadith. The Holy book Quran, the primary source of Islamic Law gives tremendous rights to man kind. The original sources forming principles and ordinances of Islam are drawn from the Holy book Quran called 'Al-Quran'. Every Muslim believes that the Quran is the divine revealed book and such all positive laws originate from it, have superiority over men made laws. "It is the real foundation on which the wide superstructure of Islam rests". It is the only absolute and final authority in every discussion relating to the principles and laws of Islam."[13] All laws, rules and principles must be in consonance with the spirit of Quran and Hadiths Anything which is contrary to the Quranic provisions or goes against Hadith will not be accepted. The Quran is in its present form is a book divided into 114 verses and consists of approximately 6666 versus in which not more than 200 verses are concerned with legal principles and nearly about 80 verses are concerned with Marriage, Dower, Divorce & etc. The Quran exercised this intl uence in different ways as :

"[1] The Quran regulates individual, social, secular and spiritual life of the Muslim.

[2] It contains the very words of God as communicated to prophet Mohammed through angel Gabriel.

[3] It has given to the world in fragmentary forms, extending over a period of 23 years

[4] It originally hadfor its objects .-

[i] repealing objectionable customs, such as usually, unlimited polygamy and gambling etc.

[ii] effecting social reforms, such as raising the status of women and equitable division of the matters of inheritance and succession. "

The Prophet Mohammad during his lifetime pronounced his verdicts, did certain things and also allowed tacitly the doing of certain things permitted by the Islam. Consequently, "what is said or done or upheld in silence by the Prophet Mohammad" becomes a primary source of Islamic Law second in point of time and authority only to the pious Quran and technically known as Sunnat. The Sunna means the model behaviour of the Prophet Mohammad. The narration of "what the Prophet Mohammad said, did or tacitly allowed" is called Hadith or tradition. At the time of his death, the Quran supplemented by Sunnat framed the whole body of Mohammadan Law - Civil, Criminal and Religious. The importance of Hadith as an important source of Islamic law has been laid down in the Quran itself. The Quran says : -

"Whatever the Prophet Mohammad gives accept it, and whatever he forbids you abstain from it. "

There are two types of Traditions mainly:

[1] Sunnat

[2] Ahadith

These two have been classified into the following three classes on the basis of the mode or manner in which it has actually originated:-

[i] Sunnat-ul-faid - traditions about the prophet did himself.

[ii] Sunnat-ul-qual - traditions about which he enjoined by words.

[iii] Sunnat-ul-tuqrir - the things done in his presence without his disapproval.

These classes of Ahadith are mentioned above :

[i] Ahadith-i-mutwabi - traditions, that are of public and universal propriety and are held as absolutely authentic. In such Hadith the chain is complete.

[ii] Ahadith-i-Mashoor - traditions which though known to a majority of people, do not possess the character of universal property.

[iii] Ahadit-e-wahid - traditions which depend on isolated individuals. "

The law is some thing living and changing. Social values are subject to constant changes and these changes affect law. The aim of the law is to fulfil the needs of society. Thus the principle of Ijma is based upon the following texts:

"God will not allow his people to agree on an error and whatever Muslims hold to be good is good before God."

With the passing of time, development of civilisation and the expansion of the Islamic influence, numerous problem arose which could not be decided by reference to only Quran and Ahadiths. The jurists therefore, evolved the principle of Ijma, The laws are needed for the benefit of the community, therefore, the divine legislator has delegated power to lay down laws by the resolution of those men in the community who are competent in that behalf that in Mujtahids or jurists. Since the Muslim religion does not admit the possibility of further revelation after the death of the Prophet Mohammad, the principle of Ijma is the only authority for legislation in the present Muslim system.

The last primary source to know Islamic Law is Qiyas. It means reasoning by analogy from the above three sources the Quran, the Sunnat, and the Ijrna, In Qiyas rules are deduced by the exercise of reason. Thus, Qiyas may be defined as a process of deduction by which the law of the text is applied to cases, which though not covered by the language are governed by reason of the text. The Qiyas does not: purport to create new law, but nearly to apply old established principles to new circumstances. The original source from which Qiyas is deduced much be capable of being extended, that is, it should not be of any special nature. The result of Qiyas should not be inconsistent with any other verse of Quran or any established Sunna and the original order of the Quran & Hadlith to which the process of Qiyas is applied should not have been abrogated or repealed. Any Qiyas must not be such as to involve a change in the law embodied in the text. In deciding legal issues, Prophet Mohammad himself relied on the Quran and on the Qiyas. The Instruction to Mu'adh-Ibn-Jabal clearly shows how he approved Qiyas in deciding legal issues. The

Qiyas was upheld by the Prophet Mohammad both by precept and practice.

The Islamic Law is also occasionally supplemented by Urf or customs and other relevant sources. The Muslim Law which prevails in India comes from these other sources too. The Islamic Law includes many rules of Pre-Islamic Customary Law, which have been embodied in it by express or implied recognition. Abdur Rahim says[14] "The ground work of Mohammedans legal system like that of any other legal system is to be found in the customs and usage of the people among whom it grew and developed. It is laid down in Hedaya that custom holds the same rank as Ijma in the absence of an express text and in another place in the same book custom is spoken of as being arbiter of analogy. It is of the very essence of custom that it should be territorial so that custom of one country cannot affect the general law of other countries. Abdur Rahim says "Further it has authority only so long as it prevails, so that the custom of one age has not force in another age.

In this regard the Shariat Act, 1937 aims at restoring the law of Islam to all Muslim Communities residing in India and abolishing customs contrary to the Shariat. This act is applicable to every Muslim irrespective of the school to which he or she belongs.

The judicial decisions also play a vital role in interpreting the Islamic Law. These include the decisions of Privy Council, Supreme Court as well as the different High Courts of the India. In deciding particular cases the judges enunciate what the law is? These decisions are regarded as precedents for further cases. These judicial decisions declare the law only and they do not work as source if law in concern with Islamic Law but these decisions supplement and modify the law. In India various legislation's have been passed either by parliament or by state legislatures to govern The Muslims Usurious Loans Act 1918, The Religious Toleration Act, The Freedom of Religions Act, 1913, The Musalman Wakf Validating Act, 1930, The Wakf Act, 1954, The Child Marriage Restraint Act, 1929, The Indian Contract Act, 1872 have affected, supplemented, and modified the Islamic Law. In 1986" an Act i.e. The Muslim 'Women (Protection of Rights on Divorce) Act, 1986 to provide separate law in respect of divorced Muslim women was enacted by the Indian Parliament.

Since, Islamic Law has been derived from the Quran, the Sunnah, Ijma, Qiyas, Istihsan, Islamic Interpretation or Ijtihad etc. serves as a medicine in deducing rules from these sources. Towards the end of the Abbasid period, however, jurists declared the door of interpretation was closed, due to the absence of qualified persons competent to make Ijtihad, and a belief that the exposition of principles by four Sunni schools was sufficient to meet all the future requirements. Ijtihad [interpretation] applied more extensively by the Imamiyah Shias than by the follower of the Sunni School. In the Shias, the door of interpretation has always been wide open and still is.

The Islam not only as a religion but as a way of life teaches that the relations of a man with his wife and children must be based on justice, charity love and fraternity." It seeks to elevate human beings inculcating in them higher spiritual values. It taught men that "the noblest of you in the sight of Allah is the best in conduct." Once these higher values are firmly established in society, the women will no longer be looked down upon because of her weakness. This is the only way to achieve symmetry and harmony in the society."

The attitude and practice of Muslim men are the factors contributing to the perpetuation of the inferior status of women in their community. Most of the men believe that the women should not have equal status with men and they don't have a right to demand a respectable life and this belief is translated into actual practice through several institutions, customs and practices which are nurtured by them. Thus, in the matter of education of girls, seclusion, payment of dower, family decision making, women's property rights, the vast majority of men either actually practice methods or at least nourish attitudes with undermined women status in the society giving them an unsecured life. These people approve the arbitrary power of divorce to wife. To be sure, the vast majority of these men know that their attitudes and practices in these matters do not have the support of the Quran or the Hadith nevertheless; they continue their behalf and practices. As a result, these beliefs and practices have hardened into traditions, customs and institutions and have found a place in the value system of the Muslim community. The present problem of women's security in the Muslim society is the result of these elements, though they have no basis in Islamic religion. Now it becomes necessary that men and young boys are informed about women's rights because in their lives they have many women around them in role of their mothers, sisters, wives, and daughters. If these women's rights are protected, the day is not a when Muslim women's right will be protected by community and state as well.

The whole study has been divided and enumerated as follows: -

- Chapter first deals with the applicability and sources of Muslim Law. With the application of Muslim Law, both the classical and modern sources of Islamic Law have been classified and analysed. The general introduction of problem has also been discussed in this chapter.
- The concept of institution of marriage has been analysed with the concept of divorce in chapter second to understand further studies of the concept of Mahr and Maintenance, because the institution of marriage constitutes the foundation of personal, family and community relationships. It is the back bone of social system in the society of the Islam. The Islamic approach accepts marriage as an essential requirement for the well-being of individual.
- In chapter third meaning, nature and essential conditions of Mahr have been discussed at length. In analysing the nature of the dower judiciary has also taken the view that dower is a necessary incident of marriage and is a debt and taken of respect to a wife.
- The classification of Mahr has been discussed in chapter fourth while quantum and Enforcement of Mahr have been discussed in chapter fifth. Different factors for determining Mahr, increase or decrease of Mahr and enforcement of Mahr will be the sub-division of this chapter.

- Chapter sixth is devoted to wife's right of retention and the nature of Mahr as an unsecured debt. Whether the right of retention in lieu of dower debt by widow is transferable and heritable is investigated. Regarding the transferability judicial opinion is not steeled even today and the controversy still exists. However, the Supreme Court had settled the controversy in respect of heritability and settled that right of retention in lieu of dower debt is heritable.
- Chapter seventh deals with "Maintenance and Muslim Women." A subject of intense controversy in the judicial decisions, in the parliament and among the public maintenance of widow and divorcee have been also discussed. Different decisions and The Muslim Women [Protection of rights on Divorce] Act, 1986, have been discussed in a very detailed manner.
- The Judicial and Legislative view relating to maintenance and the various decisions afterwards of Shah Bano's case have been discussed in chapter eight and further the legislature development in this regard have also been analysed.
- In chapter ninth, law of Inheritance in respect of Muslim women has been discussed with reference to the general principles of inheritance law.
- The conclusive observations and suggestions, which are submitting by the researcher, in chapter tenth as "Conclusion and Suggestions."

Reference:-

1 The Oman – IV, I (Sura - at - Nisa)

2 The (Juran - IV. 32 (Sura - al - Nisa)

3 The Quran - III. 195 (Sura - al-Tmran)

4 The Quran - XIV. 31 (Sura - Lukrnan)

5 Ibn-e-Maja, Surman : The Rook of Al-Adab

6 Bukhari. AI - Sahib

7 The Quran - XXX. 21 (Sura - al - Rum)

8 The Quran - IV, 9 (Sura - al - Nisa)

9 Fyzee - A Modern Approach to Islam

10 Anderson - Significance of Islamic Law in the World Today

11 Islam and the Modern Age: An Analysis and An Appraisal

12 Islam - The Misunderstood Religion

13 Ahmed Mansoor Hanaf - A survey of Islam. Institution and Culture

14 Abdul Rahim - Principal of Mohammadan Jurisprudence

CHAPTER-II

CHAPTER-II
The Historical Background and the Concept of Mahr and Maintenance

(a) Mahr and the concept of Muslim Marriage

All man kind are one,
and mutual rights,
must be respected,
the sexes must honour,
each the other;
Sacred are family relationships
that rise through marriage
and woman bearing children:
Orphans need especial loving care.[1]

What can be holier cement to:
Than that woman should be chaste
and pure and crimes against sex rooted out ?
Let decency kindness,
and justice prevail on all sex relationships,
Let marriage be cherished and carefully guarded;
women's rights secured:
Adjusted: and all life lived,

In faith. Charity, and kindness sincere,
To all our fellow-creatures.[2]

To analyse the historical background of Mahr in a true manner it is necessary to study the concept of marriage first. Both the concepts are co-related. There is a marriage, there is a Mahr. There can be no marriage without Mahr. Here it is very important to go through the history of the institution of marriage before going to elaborate the different laws related to Muslim marriage. The family law had no existence before. The Holy Prophet Mohammed and because there was no general law of races inhibiting the Arabian Peninsula, each tribes was governed by its own laws and matter in disputes were referred to the chief or decided by and appeal to the word. Those were the days of superstition and idolatry. The position of woman was not much better then that of animal. They had no legal rights, in youth they were the goods and chattels of the father and after marriage the husband became the lord and master. Polygamy was universal, divorce was easy and female infanticide was common. This was the condition of the Arabian society in which reforms were introduced by the Islam to bring about a complete transformation of the society. The Arabs themselves were so much conscious of this change that they began to refer to the period before Prophet Mohammed as the Ayyam-il-Jahiyya i.e. the period of ignorance or rather wildness, or savagery in contrast to the moral reasonableness of a civilized man. Before the Islam, Tribes and the Chieftains acted in accordance with tradition and convention. Ancient Arabian custom regulated the relations between the sexes and filiations of children. Marriage in regular form and, and with this system various other connection between members of the opposite sex were common.

Abdur Rahim, describes four types of Arabian marriages prevailing before the Islam :

I. A form of marriage similar to that sanctioned by Islam, that a man would ask another for the hand of his daughter or ward and then marry her by giving her a certain dower.

II. A man desiring noble off spring would ask his wife to send for a great chief and have intercourse with him. During the period of such intercourse the husband would stay away, but return to her after pregnancy was well advanced.

III. A number of men, less than ten, would be invited by a woman to have intercourse with her. If she conceived, and was delivered of a child, she had the right to summon all the man and they were bound to come. She would then say '0 so and so, this is your son'. This established paternity conductively and the man had no right to disclaim it.

IV. Common prostitutes were well known. They used to have definite number of visitors and their tents had a special tlag as a sign of their calling. If a woman of this class conceived, the men who frequently visited her house were assembled and the physiognomies decided to whom the child belonged.

The temporary marriage (Muta) was a common practice and from a study of Hadith it would be seen that Muta was a form of legalized prostitution tolerated by the Prophet Mohammed in the earlier days of the Islam but later on he prohibited it. In modern acceptation of the term some of conjugal relations described above can not be called marriages. It is more appropriate today to consider them as forms of legalized prostitution or of tribal sexual behavior recognized by custom. The Prophet Mohammed forbade all these types of marriage and he also forbade the Muta marriages. In paganism the idea of sale of the woman was connected with the marriage and the Islam adopted this concept and reformed it by making the woman the principal contracting party as well as the object of the contract and the present forum of the marriage.

Quranic Injunctions regarding Marriage

In the first place it would be appropriate to mention here, that what the Quran has to say in connection with marriage because the Quran is a supreme and basic source of the Islamic Law.

Sura-2; Ayat-235 - There is no blame on you that you make them an offer of marriages. It does not make a secret contract except in terms honorable, nor is resolve on the time of marriage till the term prescribed fulfilled.

Sura-5; Ayat-6 - Lawful unto in marriages all only chaste woman who are believers but chaste woman among the people of the book revealed before your time when you give them their due dowers and desire chastity not lewdness nor secret intrigues.

Sura-4; Ayat-25 to 29 - If any of you have not the means where with to marry free believing woman they may wed believing maidens, marry with the permission of their people and give them their dues, they being chaste, and met formicating and not receiving paramours.

Sura-33; Ayat-50 - We have made lawful to three wives to whom thou has paid their dowers. And daughter of the paternal uncles and aunts and daughters of the maternal uncles and aunts and any believing woman.

Sura-24; Ayat-221 - The prohibited Class - Do not marry unbelieving woman until they believe............ Nor marry your girls to unbelievers until they believe.

Sure-4; Ayat-22 to 24 - The prohibited classes and not marry those women whom your fathers married - Except what is past; it was shameful and odious, and abominable custom indeed. Prohibited to you are your mothers, daughters, sisters fathers, sisters brothers daughters sisters daughters foster mothers (who gave you suck) foster sisters, your wives mothers, your step daughters under your guardianship born wives ye have gone in, no prohibition if you have not gone in wives of your sons proceeding from your lions; and two sisters in wedlock at one and the same time except for what is past also prohibited are women already married except for these all others are lawful provided you seek them (in marriage) with gifts from your property desiring, chastity not lust give them their dower as prescribed.

Sure-24; Ayat-3 - Let no man guilty of adultery or fornication many any but a woman similarly guilty. To the believers such a thing is forbidden.

Sura-2; Ayat-282 - Nikahnama as Contract - O ye who believe when ye deal with each other in transactions involving future obligations, reduce them to writing, let a scribe write down faithfully as between the parties; let him who incurs the liability dictate, but let him fear lord God and diminish aught of what he owes, if the party liable is mentally deficient or week or unable himself to dictate let his guardian dictate faithfully and get two witnesses out of your own men, and if there are not two men, then a man and two women, such as you choose for witnesses; it is juster in the right of God, more suitable as evidence and more convenient to prevent doubts among yourselves.

Sura-3; Ayat-3 - Number of wives - If ye fear that ye shall not be able to deal justly with the orphans (orphan wives) and their property. Marry woman of your choice, two or three or four, but if you fear that ye shall not be able to deal justly (with them) then only one woman that would be more suitable to prevent you from doing injustice.

Sura-4; Ayat-35 - Obligation of husbands - Men are protectors and maintainer of woman.

Sura-4; Ayat-10 - General behavior with women - "0 ye who believe you are forbidden to inherit women against their will. Nor shall you beat them with harshness on the contrary line with them on a footing of kindness and equity. If ye take a dislike to them it may be that ye dislike (only) one thing, and God brings about through it a great deal good. On the above mention verses of the Holy Quran it is clear that for Muslim marriage is the element of chastity not for lust, age, similarly, consent, and Sadaqa to the wife is essential.

Marriage in the eye of Hadith

In order to understand the actual nature of Muslim marriage various traditions ordained by The Holy Prophet Mohammed to the followers of the Islam are given below:-

The Prophet Mohammed says, "Nikah is my Sunnah (tradition). "He directed to be faithful to the contract the marriage in Mosque and propagate others to same effect. In order to enhance and maintain its sanctity as the Mosque are the most sacred place before the God. Any person who does not marry for fasting, praying and keeping himself awake in the night has been scolded by the Prophet Mohammed. I keep fast, and break it, I pray and I sleep and I am married so whoever inclined to any other way then by my Sunnah, he is not of me. The Prophet Mohammed said that when a man marriage truly, he perform half his religion. It is now rests with him to complete the other half by leading a virtuous life in constant fear of the God. There is no act of worship except marriage and faith which is continued from the date of Adam and which will continue in paradise as well. 6 assembly of youths whoever among you is to have, he should marry for, it is restraint to the look and he who not able to do let him keep fast. There are three persons whom the Almighty himself has undertaken to help first, who seek by buy his freedom. Second, who marries with a view of secure his chastity and third, who fights in the cause of the God. Whoever marries a woman in order that he may retain his eyes - the God put blessedness in her and in him for her? The Prophet Mohammed is reported by some of the writers to say that marriage is equal to Jihad. It is sinful not to perform marriage. It is Sunnah, it is obligatory on those who are physically fit and afford it.

Now, if marriage is nothing but a civil contract then keeping in view the above traditions, he who enters into civil contract completes half of his religion. The Almighty God himself undertake to help the person who enters into civil contract is equal to Jihad. It is obligatory to very physically fit Muslim to enter into a civil contract, and so on. All these inferences patent absurdities and are untenable, which means Muslim marriage is something more than a civil contract. The Prophet Mohammed has also recommended the prayer to the God for divine blessing at the first meeting of husband and wife. In the light of recommendations of the Quran and Hadith it is clear as to what is the object of marriage. The object of Muslim marriage is the preservation of human species, the fixing of descent, restraining men for debauchery, the promotion of love, affection and union between the husband and wife, mutual help in earning livelihood, protection and encouragement of chastity and not mere gratification of sexual lust and procreation of children. The union which the marriage denotes is really of two souls which are essentially one. If they remain separate, then it will give rise to an unnatural state of affairs. When unite by way of marriage, they enter into a natural state, as such union is necessary for their physical, mental, emotional and social well being. The people enjoined to marry as it is necessary to lead a virtuous life where immorality does not find any place and mutual pledge so taken is necessary for mutual conform, protection and to effectively play the role assigned to the male and female in the society of Islam in this regard The Quran states:

.... (your wives)

They are your garments,

And ye are their garments,[3]

This clearly establishes the fact that both husband and wife are assigned an equal role within their respective sphere in shaping their behavior according to the rights and duties imposed upon them in sphere of human relationships. Further, According to Imam Muslim, Sahih Muslim mutual effect is indicated to the spirit which is to guide them in all their actions, spiritual, moral and social and this union of sexes is not merely temporary relationship but is designed as permanent and enduring alliance and both the partners are directed to make earnest effort to live in harmony and to discharge their responsibilities in a satisfactory manner so as to oust conflict and dissension from their married life. In case they act according to the code of behavior as laid down in the book, they are promised equal rewards. A woman is not a play thing but a spiritual and moral being who on the basis of sacred pledge is to provide man with a co-partners for making the life of salves, that of the family and ultimately of the whole humanity significantly meaningful. It is a social institution will well defined rights and duties incumbent upon the spouses.

Definition of Marriage

As a word of Arabic language 'Nikah' is a wide term, comprising many different forms of sex relationship, but in Muslim

Law it has a very definite legal meaning. It is a contract for the legalization of intercourse and the procreation of children. Here, below are some definitions of various scholars in regard with 'Nikah' the Muslim marriage.

Hedaya- " Nikah in its primitive sense, means carnal conjunction.

Some have said that is signifies conjunction generally. In the language of the law it implies a particular contract used for the purpose of legalizing generation. "

Ameer Ali[4] -" Marriage is an institution ordained for the protection of society, and in order that human beings may guard themselves from foulness and unchastely."

Justice Mahmood:[5] -" Marriage among Mohammedans is not a sacrament but purely a civil contract."

M.U.SJung:[6] -" Marriage though essentially a contract is also a devotional act, its objects are the right of enjoyment, procreation of children and the regulation of social life in the interest of the society."

Abdur Rahim[7]- " The Mohammedan jurists regard the institution of marriage as partaking both of the nature of Ibabat or devotional acts and Muamlat or dealings among men."

Among all above definitions, it is submitted that Abdur Rahim definition can be considered the most balanced one, by using the two ingenious words "Ibadat" and "Muamlat" he has summarised the whole concept of Muslim marriage in one sentence.

Legal incidents of a Valid Marriage

In Islam the legal incidents of marriage are remarkable for their extreme simplicity. The marriage may be constituted without any ceremonial and there are no special rites, no proper officiates, no irksome formalities are required. The essential requirements are Ijab (offer) and Qubul (acceptance). In Ameer Ali's words[8], the essential conditions of a valid marriage may be summarised that Ijab (offer), Qubul (acceptance) Baligh (adult age / puberty), Rashid (sound mind, not Majnum or non-compos mentis) parties i.e. groom and bride or when minor their guardians, two witnesses (in Hanafi Law, not Shia Law), and same meeting (i.e. at one session complete). The completion of this contract which commences with proposal or demand in marriage ends with the consent is called' Aqd'.

Forms of Muslim Marriage

As to the forms, the following conditions are necessary :_

(i) Offer on the part of one party to the marriage.

(ii) Acceptance by the other party.

(iii) Presence of two witnesses, where the parties are Hanafis and no witnesses are required, if the parties are Shias.

(iv) The words with which the marriage is contracted must be cl!ear and unambiguous.

(v) The proposal and acceptance must both be expresses in one and the same meeting.

(i) Declaration of offer (Ijab) on the part of one side ; (ii) acceptance (Qubul) by the other (or by guardians, as the case may be);

and (iii) before sufficient witnesses (In Hanafi Law, two and in Shia Law witnesses are not necessary)[9] & (iv) The words must indicate with reasonable certainty that a marriage has been contracted. There must be no ambiguity, no question of an intention to marry, nor a mere promise to marry at some future time. As in other contracts, there must be 'per vera de praesenti not de futuro' and as Arabic has only two tenses, the perfect and the aorist, ambiguity is avoided by the use of the perfect. In other words, verbally, the contract must be completed at one and the same time and place. Wilson[10] observes that in order to distinguish an actual contract of marriage from a mere promise to marry, it is necessary that the words of proposal and acceptance should be such as to show an intention to establish the conjugal relation from the moment of acceptance. The usual form of proposal is 'I have married myself to you'; the acceptance being 'I have married myself to you'; the acceptance being 'I have consented' not 'I am marrying' or 'will marry' etc. or an offer may be in the imperative 'marry your daughter to me' and the father accepts in the perfect tense 'I have consented'. The proposal and acceptance must both be expressed at one meeting; a proposal made at one meeting and an acceptance at another meeting does not constitute a valid marriage. A mere betrothal does not create any rights in Muslim Law and different ceremonies and customs which prevail in each marriage can be distinguished from the requirements of law.

Fitzgerald mentions three customs usually prevail in Muslim marriage:

(a) A marriage feast in generally given by the bridegroom; this is supposed to be almost a religious duty.

(b) The presence of one or more Waki is (agents) to represent each side is customary. They settle the details of the treaty of marriage.

(c) The Qazi is ordinarily present. The Qazi in India is the mere keeper of a marriage register and his function is purely evidentiary. It is a mistake to suppose that he joins the couple in marriage; the marriage takes effect by operation of law on the contract being completed between the parties.

As far as the question of witnesses is concern, reference can be made Mst.Ghulam Kubra Vs. Mohammad Shafi[11] The description of typical marriage ceremony was given in this case by Mir Ahmed J. in instructive and interesting both and it is the matter of every day occurrence with minor local variations. He says, according to Muslim Law, it is absolutely necessary that the man or someone on his behalf and the woman or someone on her behalf should agree to the marriage at one meting and the agreement should be witnessed by two adult witnesses. As women are in Pardah in this part of the country it is customary to send a relation of the woman to her inside the house accompanied by two witnesses. The relation asks the girl within the hearing of the witnesses whether she authorizes him to agree to the marriage on her behalf for the dower money offered by the husband. He explains to her the detail of the dower proposed. When the girl says 'yes' or signifies her consent by some other method, the three persons come out. The future husband and those three persons are then placed before the Mullah. The Mullah asks the boy whether he offers to marry the girl on payment of the specified dower. He says 'yes', then the relation, who had gone inside, tells the Mullah that he is the agent of the girl. The Mullah asks him whether she agrees to the marriage on payment of the specified dower. The relation says 'yes'. The witnesses are present there so that if the Mullah has any doubt he should question them as to whether relation is duly authorized agent of the girl. Directly both sides have said 'yes' the Mullah reads scriptures and the marriage is complete.

Capacity

Every Muslim of sound mind who has attained majority can enter into a contract of marriage. The majority is attained at puberty. The presumption is that a person attains majority 15, but the Hedaya lays down that the earlier period for a boy is 12 years and for a girl 9 years. The Privy Council in a Shiite case says that majority in the case of a girl is attained at the age of 9.[12] The marriage of minors can be contracted only by their guardians. Such a marriage, although valid, is capable of being repudiated. In a decision it was decided that a marriage entered into by a girl while she had not attained puberty was not a marriage in the eye of the law, and was therefore void.[13]

Khyar-ul-Bulugh (Option of Puberty)

A Muslim minor has been married during minority by a guardian, the minor has the right on attaining majority to repudiate such marriage. This is called Khyar-ul-Bulugh, the option of puberty.

Such a minor may be given in marriage either (1) by the father or grandfather or (2) by any other guardian. As per the older law, a minor girl contracted in marriage by her father or grandfather could not exercise the option of puberty; this restriction has now been removed by statute.[14] Such an option can only be exercised by the wife, if she files a substantive suit under the Act; it cannot be exercised by her in a suit by her husband for restitution of conjugal rights or in any other proceedings. But in Madhya Pradesh the view has been taken that the wife can exercise the option even in a suit filed by the husband for restitution.[15] In the case of girl married during minority, she is entitled to dissolution of her marriage if she proves the following facts. First, that she was given in marriage by her father or other guardian; Secondly, that the marriage took place before she attained the age of 15; Thirdly, that she repudiated the marriage before she attained the age of 18; and Fourthly, that the marriage has not been consummated. Consummation of marriage before the age of puberty does not deprive the wife of her option. The clause (vii) of Section 2 of the Act, 1939 fixes 15 years as the age of puberty without any opportunity of rebuttal. This clause does not speak of puberty at all, but only of an age, though in fact it deals within the option arising at puberty, and the only way it can be reasonably interpreted is that a woman who has before the age of 15 years been given away in marriage by her guardian is allowed to repudiate her marriage for a period of 3 years after she attains the age of 1 5 years and before she attains the age of 18 years. The husband, married during minority has the same right to dissolve his marriage, but in his case there is no statutory period of time within which he must exercise his right. The option can be exercised on his attaining majority, and payment of dower or cohabitation implies ratification. The right of repudiation is lost, first on consummation. It has been held, however, that a wife's right is not determined by mere consummation if she was ignorant of her right. Secondly, the right is also lost in the case of a female if on attaining puberty and on being informed of the right, she does not repudiate the marriage within a reasonable time. By the statue, the wife must exercise the option before she attains the age of 18 years. The mere exercise of the option to repudiate does not sever the marital tie. The repudiation must be confirmed by a court; until that time, the marriage subsists, and if one of the spouses dies, the other has the right to inherit from him or her. The High Court of Lahore (West Pakistan) has decided that a court's decree is not necessary to sever the marital tie; but High Court of Madhya Pradesh has held that a decree of the court is necessary.

Disabilities

There are seven main limitations to the unfettered capacity for a Muslim to marry any person of the opposite sex. The prohibition may be on the grounds of (1) Number; (2) Religion; (3) Relationship (Consanguinity, Affinity & Fosterage); (4) Unlawful Conjunction; (5) Idda & (7) Miscellaneous Prohibitions.

(1) Number

As to plurality of husbands or wives the rule in Islamic Law is that a Muslim man may marry any number of wives not exceeding four but a Muslim woman can marry only one husband, if a Muslim marries a v" wife, such marriage is not void but irregular whereas if a Muslim woman marries a second husband she is liable for bigamy Under Section 494 Indian Penal Code, the of Is pring of such a marriage are illegitimate and cannot be legitimated by any subsequent acknowledgement.

(2) Religion

The difference of schools - Muslims belonging to different schools may intermarry freely with one another and a mere difference of school of law, such as Shiite or Sunnite, Hanifi or Shafi, is entirely immaterial. Each spouse retains his or her own status on marriage, and no rule of law compels the wife to adopt the husband's school; there is thus no mergence as in the law of domicile.

Difference of Religion

A man in Hanafi Law may marry a Muslim woman or a Kitabiyya ; but a Muslim woman cannot marry anyone except a Muslim. It is necessary to explain the terms Kitabi and Kitabiyya, the former of which refers to a man and the latter to a woman. A Kitabi is a man believing in a revealed religion possessing a Divine Books. The words Kitabi and Kitabiyya have also been rendered 'scipturary'. In India, it is a term applied only to Jews and Christians, each of whom possess a revealed book (Kitabi), but it really extends to the adherents of other religions also for instance to Samaritans, Sabaeans and, according to the Ithna Ashari and Fatimid Shiites, to the Zoroastrians as well. The question arose before the Privy Council, whether a Buddhist can be regarded as a scripturary or not. But when it was proposed to examine and discuss the tenants of Buddhism with a view to showing that Buddhists come under the same category as Jews and Christians, with whom Muslims could undoubtedly intermarry, their lordships declined to entertain that question in the circumstances of that case.[16] Thus, it remains an open question. A Muslim, however, cannot marry an idolatress or a fire worshipper; and a Muslim woman cannot even marry a Kitabi, except in India under the Special Marriage Act, 1954. The rule among the Shiites is very strict. A Shiite, whether male or female, cannot marry a non Muslim in the Nikah (or permanent) form; but he can contract a Muta marriage with a Kitabiyya (including afire worshipper) As the Fatimids hold that Zoroastrians (Majus) belong to the group designated as Ahl-i-Kitab, a man belonging to that school can marry a Zoroastrian female lawfully though a Fatimid woman cannot lawfully marry a Zoroastrian man.

The question arises; what is the position if a marriage prohibited on the ground of religion does take place? It is to be treated as entirely void (Batil) or merely irregular (Fasid) ? Ameer Ali[17] has argued eloquently that an examination of the law reveals a basic misconception in this branch. He is of opinion that 'A Muslim may, therefore, lawfully intermarry with a woman belonging to the Brahmo-Sect. Nor does there seem to be any reason why a marriage with a Hindu woman whose idolatry is merely nominal and who really believes in God should be unlawful. The Moghul Emperors of India frequently intermarried with Rajput (Hindu) ladies and the issue of such unions were regarded as legitimate and often succeeded to the imperial throne. He therefore, proceeds to lay down that such unions are merely irregular, and not void, for example when a Mohammedan marries a Hindu woman, the marriage is only invalid (irregular, according to our nomenclature) and does not affect the legitimacy of the offspring, as the polytheistic woman may at any time adopt the Islam which would at once remove the bar and validate the marriage. He shows that the rules as to difference of religion or apostasy were based on the principle of political safety. Infidelity implied hostility to the commonwealth of the Islam and apostasy was tantamount to treason. These conditions no longer exist and he pleads for a more liberal view. Whether the courts would, in view of the clear texts of law and Quranic provisions, accept such a broad view in all its implications is extremely doubtful, but Tyabji[18] says, "The present conditions of life conduce to marriages between persons of different religions and it is not unlikely that the legislature may step in and validate such marriages between persons of different religions and it is not unlikely that the legislature may step in and validate such marriages." This has been now done in India by the Special Marriage Act, 1954 where a civil marriage can take place. The present position appears to be that the Nikah of a Muslim man with an idolater or fire worshipper is irregular and not void. Mulla goes on to say, however, that the marriage of a Muslim woman with a non Muslim is only irregular, not void. This is, it is submitted, an inaccurate statement of the law. The marriage of a Muslim woman with a non-muslim is declared by the Holy Quran to be Batil, void and not merely irregular. Thus it would seem that reform, in consonance with the view of Ammer Ali, can only be introduced by legislation. In India a Muslim can lawfully marry to a Jewish or Christian woman according to the tents of Mohammedan Law. If a Muslim marries a Jewish the union is valid according to Mohammedan Law, but as all religions are equal before the law the Jewish Law on the point, obviously a complication would arise if such a union is valid according to the law applicable to one party but no according to the law applicable to the other. If the husband took action against her, and she denied the validity of the marriage, but she can deny in the garb of applicable law, what would be the result? No such case seems to have occurred in India. But it is submitted that in such a case the court would decide in accordance with the law of the defendant. Marriages between Muslims and Christians have been fairly frequent. A Muslim woman cannot marry a Christian; such a union would be void but a Muslim may marry a Christian woman in accordance with Mohammedan Law. Such a marriage must in India be solemnized in accordance with the provisions of the Indian Christian Marriage Act, 1872. The marriage of a Christian must take place in present of marriage registrar, else it would be void. Since a Muslim woman cannot lawfully marry a non-muslim, she can not be married to a Christian under the provisions of this Act.

Civil Marriage

It is necessary to add that the above discussion applies only in the case of Nikah according to Mohammedan Law, and not to a civil marriage in India under the Special Marriage Act 43 of 1954. This Act provides for a marriage between any two persons, regardless of religion, provided that neither party has a spouse living neither party is an idiot or a lunatic the male has completed the age of twenty one years and the female in the age of 18 years the parties are not within the degrees of prohibited relationship and where the marriage is solemnized outside India, both parties are citizens of India and domiciled in India. This Act provides in Section 15-18 for the registration of other forms of marriage. Upon such registration the most important consequence for a Muslim is that succession to the property of such person and his issue is regulated by the Indian Succession Act, 39 of 1925.

(3) Relationship.

(A) Consanguinity:- The third bar to marriage is on the ground of blood relationship. A man is prohibited from marrying:

(i) his mother or grand mother how high so ever;

(ii) his daughter or grand daughter how low so ever; (iii) his sister whether full consan give uterine;

(iv) his niece or great niece how low so ever;

(v) his aunt or great-aunt how high so ever, paternal or maternal.

A marriage with a woman prohibited by reason of blood relationship is totally void and the issue is illegitimate.

(B) Affinity: - A man is also prohibited from marrying certain relations by affinity. These are (i) ascendants or descendants of his wife; and (ii) the wife of any ascendant or descendant. By way of exception, a man may marry the descendant of a wife with whom the marriage has not been consummated. A marriage prohibited on the ground of affinity is generally declared to be void.

(C) Fosterage: - Where the relationship of fosterage is established, Mohammedan Law prohibits the marriage within certain limits. A man may not, for instance, marry his foster-mother, or her daughter, or his foster-sister. A marriage forbidden by reason of fosterage is void.

(5) Unlawful Conjunction.

A man is also forbidden to have two wives at the same time, so related to each other by consanguinity, affinity & fosterage that they could not have lawfully intermarried with each other if they had been of different sexes. Thus a man cannot marry two sisters, or an aunt and her niece. Under Hanafi Law, generally speaking, disregard of the bar of unlawful conjunction renders the marriage irregular but not void. The most important case arising under this rule is the marriage of two sisters to one man. There is nothing to prevent a man from marrying his wife's sister after the death or divorce of his wife; but it is unlawful to marry two sisters at the same time, or to marry the sister of the wife during the wife's lifetime. The view of the Calcutta High

Court[19] guided clearly by the Quranic[20] provision and (it is forbidden unto you) that ye should have two sisters together, was that such unions were void and the issue illegitimate but the High Courts of Bombay, Madras and Lahore, and the Chief Court of Oudh have in their decisions declared them to be merely irregular and the issue legitimate. It is evident that the later decisions have been influenced by the elaborate criticism of Aizunnissa's case by Ameer Ali and as they tend to legitimise the issue of such marriages, a almost all the text writers favour them and the rule may now be said to be firmly established in India. It seems, however, necessary to insist that where a clear rule of law is found in the Quran, legislation and not 'elastic interpretation' is the proper remedy.

(6) Idda

In Mohammedan Law, when a marriage is dissolved by death or divorce, the woman is prohibited from marrying within a specified time. This period is called Idda[21] and the most approved definition of 'Idda' is the term by the completion of which a new marriage is rendered lawful. It is a period of continence imposed on a woman on the termination of a marriage in the interests of certainty of paternity during which a woman is supposed to live a life of seclusion and to abstain from certain luxuries.

(A) The observance of 'Idda' is necessary where cohabitation has taken place; such cohabitation may be lawful, as in the case of consummation of marriage is unlawful, as in illicit intercourse.

If pregnancy follows due to illicit intercourse 'Idda' must be observed.[22]

(B) If consummation of marriage has taken place and the marriage is dissolved by divorce, the duration of 'Idda' is there courses, or if the woman is pregnant, till delivery. If the marriage is dissolved by death, the period of 'Idda' is four months and ten days or, if the woman is pregnant, till delivery, whichever is longer.

(C) If consummation of marriage has not taken place 'Idda' has to be observed in the case of death, but not in the case of divorce.

Valid retirement (Al-Khalwat-al-Sahiha)

The question of consummation is, therefore, of prime importance in the law relating to 'Idda'. In certain cases 'valid retirement' has the same legal effect as consummation. When the husband and wife are alone together under circumstances which present no legal, moral or physical impediment to marital intercourse, they are said to be in 'valid retirement' or in Al-Khalwat-al-Sahiha. The Radd-al-Muhtar lays down that four conditions are necessary (i) there must be actual privacy (ii) there must not be any physical (iii) moral or (iv) legal bar. The Fatawa Alamgiri and the Radd-al-Muhtar have laid down in precise terms the cases in which valid retirement is to be treated as having the same legal effects as actual consummation. In (i) the confirmation of Mahr, (ii) the establishment of paternity (iii) the observance of 'Idda' (iv) the wife's right of maintenance and residence during 'Idda' (v) the bar of marriage with the wife's sister and (vi) the bar as to marrying four other wives beside her, valid retirement has the same effects as consummation. But mere valid retirement does not prevent marriage with the wife's daughter and, in the case of a triply divorced couple, remarriage between them is impossible unless the divorced wife is married to another husband, and duly divorced by the second husband after actual consummation. In these two cases, actual consummation is necessary, valid retirement not being sufficient. A marriage, with a woman undergoing 'Idda is irregular,' but not void. The Fatimids declared such marriage to be void.[23]

Other Prohibitions

In additions to the above mention prohibitions to marry there are few others however not so important. These are the rules of prudence rather than the mandatory provisions of law there are:

(1) Kafaa

The doctrine of equality in Marriage. This is the rule recognized by society that in order that a marriage may bear the character of a suitable union in law, the husband must be the equal of the woman in social statues. It is not necessary that the wife should be of an equal status with the husband because by marriage itself he was assumed to raise here to his own position. So the Hands hold that equality (Kafaa) between the two parties in a necessary condition in marriage. The following factors must be considered for determining equality (a) family; (b) Islam; (c) profession ;(d) freedom; (e) good character; & (f) means.

The Shafis consider slightly different qualifications from the nature of rules, it is clear that Kafaa is not so much a legal prohibition, as a rule of worldly wisdom. In Jamait Ali Saheb Vs. Mir Mohammed[24] a Punjab case it was laid down that a disregard of the rules of equality does not the marriage void ab-initio and that the court was not justified in dissolving the marriage. It is submitted that, as pointed out by Tyabji in certain circumstances the court exercising the jurisdiction of the Qazi has the power to annul such a marriage. The true nature of the rule is that it is not an absolute prohibition to marry but it allows the Qazi to rescind the marriage (Faskh) in certain cases of misalliance. It may be likened to a voidable contract.

(2) Illicit intercourse and undue familiarity

If a person has illicit intercourse with a woman or commits act of undue familiarity some of the woman's relations are forbidden to him, although he can marry the woman herself.

(3) Pilgrimage

In Ithna Ashari and Shafi Law a man who has come within the sacred precincts of the Kaba and put on the pilgrim's dress, may not enter into a contract of marriage while on the pilgrimage

(4) Divorce

Divorce constitutes an important legal bar and will be fully considered in the section on Divorce. Briefly stated, the rule is that when a man divorces a woman, and the divorce is effective as triple Talaq, remarriage between them is impossible unless the woman observes 'Idda, lawfully marries another husband, the second marriage is consummated, and the second husband lawfully and effectively divorces her. Some important cases have occurred in India and they require careful consideration.

Classifications of Marriage

(1) Valid Marriage (Sahih): or

(2) Void Marriage (Batil); or

(3) Irregular Marriage (Fasid)

(1) Valid Marriage (Sahih)

A marriage which conforms in all respects with the law is termed Sahih correct in regard to legal requirements. For a marriage to be valid it is necessary that there should be no prohibition affecting the parties. Now prohibitions may be either perpetual or temporary. If the prohibition is perpetual, the marriage is void; if temporary, the marriage is irregular.

(2) Void Marriage (Batil)

A marriage which has no legal results is termed Batil or Void. It is the semblance of marriage without the reality. A marriage forbidden by the rules of blood relationship, affinity or fosterage is void. The issue of such a union is illegitimate, and law knows no process whereby the union may be legalized. Similarly, a marriage with the wife of another, or remarriage with a divorce wife, when the legal bar still exists, is void. A void marriage is an unlawful connection which produces no mutual rights and obligations between the parties, for example - there is no right of dower, unless there has been consummation. The death of one of them does not entitle the other inherit from the deceased. The illegality of such unions commences from the date when the contracts are entered into and the marriage is considered as totally non-existing in fact as well as in law.

(3) Irregular Marriage (Fasid)

A union between a man and a woman may be either lawful or unlawful. Unlawfulness may be either absolute or relative. If the unlawfulness is absolute, marriage would be a void marriage (Batil). If it is relative than irregular marriage (Fasid).

The following marriages have been considered irregular:

(i) A marriage without witnesses;

(ii) A marriage with a woman undergoing 'Idda'

(iii) A marriage prohibited by reason of difference of religion

(iv) A marriage with two sisters, or contrary to the rules of unlawful conjunction;

(v) A marriage with a fifth wife

The Ithna Ashari and Fatimid schools of law do not recognize the distinction between void and irregular marriages. A marriage is, according to those systems, either valid or void; hence the above mentioned unions would be treated as void marriages.

Effect of an Irregular Union

As between the parties themselves, the irregular union is flimsy tie giving few rights; but as regards the issue, they are given full legal status. As far as their separation from such type of union is concern it is the duty of the Qazi to separate the spouses, but the union may be terminated also by either party at any time; neither divorce, nor the intervention of a court is necessary. One of them may say 'I have relinquished you and the unholy alliance ends. As to consummation, If there has been consummation the wife is entitled to dower, proper or specified, whichever is less, and she must observe 'Idda for three courses. As to Inheritance, No rights of inheritance are created between the husband and the wife by an irregular marriage. If the issue is treated as legitimate and is entitled to a share of the inheritance.

The 'irregular marriage' of Islam is a connection between a man and a woman which, though not amounting to a lawful marriage, confers the status of legitimacy on the children. In this respect it is similar to a Scottish or Canadian purgative marriage. The logical separation of the question of the legitimacy of the child from that of the validity of the parent's marriage was also developed by cannon law and has been accepted in English Law. It was said by the Privy Council in a case dealing with a Chiness conjugal union that 'a court may do well to recollect that it is a possible Jural conception that a child may be legitimate though its parents were not and could not be legitimately married.[25]

Legal effects of a Valid Marriage

Justice Mahmood has discussed the legal effects of a Muslim marriage in the leading case of Abdul Kadir Vs. Salima.[26] These authorities leave no doubt as to what constitutes marriage in law, and it follows that, the moment the legal contract is established, consequences flow from it naturally and imperatively as provided by the Mohammedan Law. The original text of the Fatawa-i-Alamgiri, which Mr.Baillie has translated in the form of paraphrase, at page 13 of his digest, which has been translate here literally, adopting Mr.Baillie's phraseology as for as possible. The legal effects of marriage are that it legalizes the enjoyment of either of them (husband and wife) with the other in the manner which this matter is permitted by the law; and it subjects the wife to the power of restraint, that is, she becomes prohibited from going out and appearing in public; it renders her dower, maintenance, and raiment obligatory on him; and establishes on both sides the prohibitions of affinity and the rights of inheritance, and the obligator of justness between the wives and their rights and on her it imposes submission to him when summoned to the couch; and confers on him the power of correction when she is disobedient or rebellious and enjoins upon him associating familiarly with her with kindness and courtesy. It renders unlawful the conjunction of two sisters (as wives) and of those who fall under the same category this conception of the mutual rights and obligations arising from marriage between the husband and wife bears in all main features close similarity to the Roman Law and other European systems which are derived from that law, cannot be doubted; and even regarding the power of correction, the English Law seems to resemble the Mohammedan, for even the former 'the old authorities say the husband may beat his wife and if in modern times the rigor of the law has been mitigated, it is because in England, as in this country, the criminal law has happily stepped in to give to the wife personal security which the matrimonial law does not. To use the language of the Lords of the Privy Council in the case already cited: The Mohammedan Law, on a question of what is legal cruelty between man and wife, would probably not differ materially from our own, of which one of the most recent expositions is the following: "There must be actual violence of such a character as to endanger personal health or safety, or there must be a reasonable apprehension of it." The court, as Lord Stowell said in Evans V s. Evans, has never been driven off this ground." Now the legal effects of marriage, as enumerated in the Fatawa-i-Alamgiri, come into operation as soon as the contract of marriage is completed by the proposal and acceptance; their initiation is simultaneous, and there is no authority in the Mohammedan Law for the proposition that any or all of them are dependent upon any condition precedent as to the payment of dower by the husband to the wife.[27] The legal effects of a valid marriage may be summarized in following lines:

(1) Sexual intercourse becomes lawful and the children born of the union are legitimate.

(2) The wife becomes entitled to her Mahr. (3). The wife becomes entitled to maintenance.

(4) The husband is entitled to restrain the wife's movements in a reasonable manner and to exercise marital authority.

(5) Mutual rights of inheritance are established.

(6) The Prohibitions regarding marriage due to the rules of affinity come into operation.

(7) The wife is not entitled to remarry after the death of her husband, after the dissolution of her marriage without observing 'Idda'.

(8) Where there is an agreement between the parties, entered into either at the time of the marriage or subsequent to it, its stipulations will be enforced, in so far as they are not inconsistent with the provisions of the policy of the law.

(9) A woman does not change her status on marriage. She remains subject to her own pre marital school of law. Neither the husband nor the wife acquires any interest in the property of the other by reason of marriage.

Nature of the Muslim Marriage

After this summarized study of Muslim marriage, a short discussion over the nature of Muslim marriage in necessary here. The nature of Muslim marriage is it self a controversial matter because of it unique incidents. The judgment in Abdul Kadir Vs. Salima[28] is one of those classic pronouncements of the illustrious Mr. Justice Mahmood the first Indian judge of the Allahabad High Court, which has acquired so great a reputation that its obiter dicta carries the legal sanctity of ratio decidendi. The case is one on the restitution of conjugal rights, yet Justice Mahmood's observations on:

(i) nature of marriage

(ii) husband's liability to pay dower

(iii) matrimonial rights of the husband and wife and

(vi) general rules of interpreting.

The Hanafi Law. have won universal recognition not only of various High Courts but also of the Privy Council and the Supreme Court. Describing the nature of Muslim marriage, Mahmood, J. says,

"Marriage among Mohammedans is not a sacrament, but purely a civil contract,' and though it is solemnized generally with recitation of certain verses from the Quran, yet the Mohammedan Law does not positively prescribe any service peculiar to the occasion. That it is a civil contract is manifest from the various ways and circumstances in and under which marriages are contracted or presumed to have been contracted. And though a civil contract, it is not positively prescribed to be reduced to writing, but the validity and operation of the whole are made to depend upon the declaration or proposal of the one, and the acceptance or consent of the other of the contracting parties, or of their natural and legal guardians before competent and sufficient witnesses, as also upon the restrictions imposed, and certain of the conditions required to be abided by according to the peculiarity of the case."

The above is an accurate summary of the Mohammedan Law is shown by the best authorities, and Mr.Baillie, in his digest, replying upon the texts of the Kanz, the Kifayah and the Inayah, has well summarized the law; Marriage is a contract which has for its design or objects the right of enjoyment and the procreation of children. But it was also instituted for the solace of life, and is one of the prime or original necessities of man. It is therefore, lawful in extreme old age after hope of offspring has ceased, and even in the last or death illness. The pillars of marriage, as of other contracts, are Ejab-o-Kubbol, or declaration and acceptance. The first speech, from whichever side it may precede, is the declaration, and the other the acceptance. The Hedaya lays down the same rule a to the constitution of the marriage contract, and Mr. Hamilton has rightly translated the original text: Marriage is contracted that is to say, is effected and legally confirmed by means of declaration and consent, both expressed in the preterit. Further, the Justice Mahmood could not be held to have taken the view that Muslim marriage is nothing but purely a civil contract. Yet this is precisely what he is accused of holding. When he approves of Baillie's view that marriage is also for the solace of life, he is himself highlighting another aspect of marriage, that is, its social aspect. The amount of dower which becomes payable after marriage must not be confused with consideration in the context of civil contract. Justice Mahmood himself is sounding a note of caution when he says in the same decision;

"Dower, under the Mohammedan Law, is a sum of money or other property promised by the husband to be paid or delivered to the wife in consideration of the marriage...............the dower of the

Mohammedan Law bears a strong resemblance to the denatio propter nuptias of the Romans which has subsisted in the English Law under the name of marriage settlement. In this sense and in no other can dower under the Mohammedan Law be regarded as the consideration for the connubial intercourse, and if the authors of the Arabic textbooks of Mohammedan Law have compared it to price in the contract of sale, it is simply because marriage is a civil contract under that law, and the sale is the typical contract which Mohammedan Jurists are accustomed to refer to in illustrating the incidents of other contracts by analogy "

The Justice Mahmood has said, up to this point, he can only be accused of neglecting the religious aspect of marriage, if the issue is seriously examined from the religious angle, the Muslim marriage in fact is an Ibadat (devotional act). The Prophet Mohammed is reported to have said that marriage is essential for every physically fit Muslim who could afford it. Moreover, the following traditions may also be considered.

"He who marries completes half his religion it now rests with him to complete the other half by leading a virtuous life in constant fear of God."

"There is no mockery in Islam."

"There are three persons whom the Almighty Himself has undertaken to help - first he who seeks to buy his freedom: second, he who marries with a view to secure his chastity, and third, he who fights in the cause of God."

"Whoever marries a woman in order that he may retain his eyes-God putted blessedness in her for him for her?"

The Prophet Mohammad is reported by some of the writers to say that marriage is equal to Jihad (holy war) it is sinful not to contract a marriage, it is a Sunnah, and is obligatory on those who are physically fit. Now, if marriage is nothing but a civil contract, then keeping in view the above traditions we could say: He who enters into a civil contract completes half of his religion; the Almighty Himself has undertaken to help the person who enters into a civil contract; civil contract is equal to Jihad; the person who enters into a civil contract; and so on. All these inferences are patent absurdities, and are untenable. Which means Muslim marriage is something more than a civil contract. The Muslim marriage ceases to look as purely a civil contract or a means only to procreate children. In the words of Baillie, marriage is "for the solace of life. It is therefore lawful in extreme old age after hope of offspring has ceased, and even in the last or death-illness." In the words of Ameer Ali, marriage is "for the protection of society, and in order that human beings may guard themselves from foulness and unchastely." Al-Ghazali, the famous jurist and philosopher, regards marriage as a means "of attaining nearness to the God."

In the famous case of Anis Begam Vs. Mohd. Istefa,[29] Sir Shah Sulaiman, C.J. observed "Marriage (in Islam) is not regarded as a mere civil contract, but a religious sacrament (too). Furthermore, Muslim marriage is not merely a civil contract, because;

(a) unlike civil contracts, it cannot be made contingent on a future event; and

(b) unlike civil contracts, it cannot be for a limited time, (Muta marriage is an exception and not a rule)

It has thus been seen that Abdur Rahim's definition is by far the best, as it gives proper weightage to both the aspects of marriage, namely, temporal and religious. Tahit Mahmood[30] is also of the view that marriage among the Muslims is a "solemn pact" (Mithaq-e-Ghalid) which in law takes the form of a contract (Aqd). He says that there is popular misconception that no religious significance or social solemnity attaches to a Muslim marriage and that is a mere 'civil contract'. This, he says, is not true. "Of course Islam does not regard marriage as a 'sacrament' (Sanskar) in the Hindu religious sense of the term. However, the Prophet Mohammad did describe Nikah (marriage) as his Sunnat, and those who know the socio-Iegal significance of Sunnat as recognized by Muslims can well understand what marriage means to a follower of Islam. The Quran too does not treat marriage as an ordinary contract. As a matter of fact it is only the form of Muslim marriage itself as a concept is not merely a contract. A.A.A.Fyzee[31] observes that while considering the social and legal aspects, the aspect of religion is often neglected or misunderstood

marriage partakes of the nature both Ibadat (worship) and Mamala (worldly affairs). The analysis of original sources of Islamic matrimony reveals that the creation of a pure civil contract theory in mercantile sense for the evaluation of the nature of marriage is hollow and baseless. Sacrifice oneness and unity; all these elements are terribly not present in pure civil contract theory but these all are basically present in Muslim marriage.

Muta Marriage

Amongst the Pre-Islamic Arabs, certain woman entertained men in their own tents; neither party acquiring only right over the other. The woman could dismiss the man at any time she chose, there being on either side entire freedom to terminate the relation at any time. The children belonged to her; it was in fact prostitution and nothing else. The practice was found convenient by the Pre-Islamic Arabs particularly during long travels. Muta is modification of this though it differs from Pre-Islamic institution in two respects:-

(1) The period or time is to be fixed while contracting Muta marriage.

(2) Mahr must be fixed in the contract for a Muta.

The Muta marriage is a kind of "temporary marriage" recognized in the Shia School of Mohammedan Law. The term., Muta implies 'enjoyment' or 'use' In Heffening's words it may be rendered as a 'marriage for pleasure' in its legal context. Wilson says that "it is lawful among Shias to enter into a contract of (so called) marriage for a limited period, which may be for a term of year, a month, a day or even a part of a day. The marriage dissolves of itself on the expiration of the term of marriage. If no time-limit is expressed, the marriage is presumed to be permanent. The number of wives that can be taken into Muta marriage is unlimited. The ceiling of four wives does not apply here. A Shia male may contract Muta with a Muslim, Christian,

Jewish or Parsi (fire worshipper) woman, but not with a woman following any other religion. A woman may not contract Muta with a non-muslim. The amount of dower must be specified in the contract of Muta otherwise the agreement is void. The child born of a Muta marriage is legitimate and capable of inheriting from the father. But in the absence of an express agreement, neither party to a Muta wife unless it has expressly been agreed upon. A.A.A.Fyzee says that the old Arabian custom of Muta was justified as being useful in times of war and travels. But the Prophet Mohammed prohibited it and later on Calipha Umar suppressed it ruthlessly. Among the Shias themselves, only Ithna Ashari School recognizes it, and it is rejected by every other Muslim School. The practice is not common in India, and in Lucknow, Rampur and other places where, Shia population reside; ladies of better class do not contract Muta marriage. The main conditions are necessary for a Muta marnage.

(a) As to period; Muta being a temporary marriage is essence, it is necessary that the Muta contact must specify the period of the enjoyment. The fixed period can again be extended by a new contract. It can also be presumed to be extended unless disproved, for example A marriage B under Muta from for 2 years. Even after the expiry of that period, A and B continued to life together without entering into a new contact. Living like this a child is born to them in the fourth year. The husband A dies in the fifth year. It will be presumed that the Muta had lasted for 5 years and the child was legitimate. But suppose A and B contact a Muta marriage for (i) unspecified time - that is mention of period is omitted, intentionally or unintentionally, or (ii) specified for lifetime. Will such contract result into Muta or Nikah ? According to a decision by the Hyderabad High Court[32] in both cases a permanent Nikah will result. Fyzee[33] does not agree with this. As to the second he says that fixation of a period in marriage contract destroys the concept of Nikah as understood in Islamic Law. As to the first, in his opinion the deciding factor should be intention of the parties rather than the form of the words. The Privy Council had also held in Shoharat Singh case[34] that where cohabitation of a man and a woman commenced with a Muta and there was no evidence as to the term of the marriage, the proper inference, unless disproved, would be that Muta continued during the whole period of cohabitation.

(b) As to dower; being a short term contract, the element of dower is rightly emphasized. The dower must be specified otherwise the contract is void. The wife's right to dower arises as soon as the marriage is consummated. She can claim the whole amount. But if she chooses to abandon the husband before the end of the fixed period, she must suffer a proportionate cut in the dower.

Relation between Divorce and Maintenance

Divorce is one of the institutions in the Islam, regarding which much misconception prevails, so much so that even the Islamic Law, as administered in the courts, is not free from these misconceptions.[35]

Marriage is marriage. There is no Hindu marriage, Parsi marriage, Christian marriage or Muslim marriage. Nevertheless concept of marriage differs and the really marks out the difference. The concept of marriage under Christian Law is that it is (1) sacrament (2) an indissoluble union (3) for (one) life. Similarly, under Hindu Law, the concept is that marriage is (1) sacrament (2) indissoluble union, and (3) for seven lives. As against this concept under Muslim Law the marriage is sacrosanct (sacred contract) and it is a dissoluble union. It means marriage is not only sacrament but also a civil contract, pure and simple. The terms 'pure' and 'simple' are not the terms of edifice but of legal connotations; 'pure' means free from conditions or restrictions and 'simple' means not evidenced by seal, writing or record. Thus while under Muslim Law, divorce is implicit in the marriage (control). It is not so in other legal systems because the they do not treat marriage as contract. The other legal systems have therefore reformed their matrimonial laws and included in it the divorce. Some of the Western Countries have begun to believe that there is no point in finding out as to wherefrom the bitter water of matrimonial dispute flows, the moment it starts and some of the (Western Countries) prescribe divorce on the asking. But it goes to the credit of Muslim Law only that it invented and originated Divorce on the asking in the form of Talaq. May be that Muslim Law invented and originated the Talaq a form of divorce on the asking but that does not invest any right in Muslims to misuse and abuse it grossly and with total immunity. Here it is important to clear that Islam is strongly against divorce and want divorce to be avoided as far as possible Islam has provided this remedy only for occasions in which there is no alterative but reparation. The Islam considers as enemies of the God those men who marry one woman after the other and divorce them in quick succession.

Pre -Islamic Institution.

Among almost all the nations of antiquity, divorce was regarded as a natural corollary of marital rights. Roman, Herbes, Israeliities and others all had divorce in one or other form. In Pre-Islamic Arab, the power of divorce possessed by the husband was unlimited. They could divorce their wives at any time, for any reason or without any reason. They could also revoke their divorce and divorce again as many times as they preferred. They could, moreover, if they were so inclined, swear that they would have no intercourse with their wives, though still living with them. They could arbitrarily accuse their wives of adultery, dismiss them and leave them with such notoriety as would deter other suitors; while they themselves would go exempt from any formal responsibility of maintenance or legal punishment.[36] According to Abdur Rahim at least four various types of dissolution of marriage were known in Pre-Islamic Arabia. These were Talaq III a, Zihar and Khula. A woman if absolutely separated through any of these four modes was probably free to remarry but she could not do so until some time, called the period of Iddat, had passed. It was to ascertain the legitimacy of the child. But it was not a strict rule. Sometimes pregnant wife was divorced and was married to another person under an agreement. It is interesting to note that the period of Iddat in case of death of husband then was one year.

Islamic Reforms.

The Prophet Mohammad of Islam looked upon these customs of divorce with extreme disapproval and regarded their practice as calculated to under mine the foundation of society. It was impossible, however, under the existing conditions of society to abolish the custom entirely. The Prophet Mohammad had to would the mind of uncultured and semi-barbarous community to a higher development. According to Ameer Ali the reforms of Prophet Mohammad marked a new departure in the history or Eastern Legislations. The Prophet Mohammad reported to have said with Allah, "the most detestable of all things permitted is divorce" and towards the end of his life he practically forbade its exercise by men without intervention of an arbiter or a judge.

The Quran ordains. "......... If ye fear a breach between them twain (the husband and the wife) appoint an arbiter from his folk and an arbiter from her folk.If they desire amendment, Allah will make them of one mind. "The Quran permits it partly because of some countenance to the customs and partly to enable men to get rid of an odious union. Prophet Mohammad restrained the power of divorce and gave to the woman the right of obtaining separation on reasonable grounds. Accordingly he allowed the exercise of the power of divorce to husbands under certain conditions. He permitted to divorced parties three distinct and separate periods within which they might endeavor to become reconciled; but should all attempts at reconciliation prove unsuccessful, then in the third period the final separation became effective.[37]

He pronounced "Talaq" to be the most detestable before God of all permitted things for it prevented conjugal happiness and interfered with the proper bringing up of children." Ameer Ali said that the permission (of divorce), therefore, in the Quran though it gave a certain countenance to the old customs, has to be read in the light of the Law giver's own enunciations. When it is borne in mind how intimately law and religion are connected in the Islamic system, it will be easy to understand the bearing of his words on the institution of divorce. An effective check placed by the Islam on frequent divorce and remarriage was that in case of irrevocable separation, it is essential for remarriage that the wife should marry another man, and this marriage should be consummated before divorce, and the wife should observe Iddat.

This was a measure which rendered separation rarer. Certain critics accuse this procedure as "a disgusting ordeal" and "revolting", but they ignore that among proud, jealous, and sensitive race like the Arabs, such a condition was one of the strongest antidotes for the evil. It intended to control one of the most sensitive nations of the earth by acting on the strongest feeling of their nature, the sense of honour.

Islamic Injunctions regarding Talaq

The Islam realized that for peace and happiness of a family and for protection and beneficial upbringing of children, divorce was undesirable. The Holy Quran puts strong restrictions on the divorce of woman by their husband. Inspite of the sacredness of the character of marriage life, Islam recognized the necessity in exceptional circumstances of keeping the way open for its dissolution. It is there for necessary to refer to the relevant verses of the Holy Quran, which is the primary source of Islamic Law on the relationship between the husband and the wife and divorce of wife by the husband.

Iddat

"Divorced woman shall wait concerning themselves for three monthly periods and their husbands have the better right to take them back in that period, if they wish for reconciliation."

Reconciliation

And woman shall have rights similar to the rights against them, according to what is equitable; but men have a degree over them.[38] A divorce is only permissible twice (revocable) : after that the parties should either hold together on equitable terms or separate with kindness. It is not lawful for you to take back any of your gifts (from them) except when both parties fear that they would be unable to keep the limits ordained by God. If you judge do indeed fear that they would be unable to keep the limits ordained by God, there is no blame on either of them if she gives something for her freedom (Khula).There are the limits ordained by God: so do not transgress them.[39]

Irrevocable after Third Pronouncement (Halala Safeguard)

If a husband divorces his wife (irrevocably) (third time) he cannot after that re-marry her until after she has married another husband and he has divorced her. In that case there is no blame on either of them if they re-unite; provided they feel that they can keep the limits ordained by God.[40] When ye divorce women and they fulfill the term of their (Iddat), not take them from marrying their (former) husbands, if they mutually agree on equitable terms either take them back on equitable terms or set them free on equitable terms, but do not take them back to injure them (or) to take undue advantage; if anyone does that he wrongs his own soul.[41] When ye divorce women and they fulfill the terms of their (Iddat) do not prevent them from marrying their (former) husbands, if they mutually agree on equitable terms.[42] There is no blame on you if ye divorce women before consummation or fixation of their dower : but bestow on them (a suitable gift) A gift of a reasonable amount is due from those who wish to do the right thing[43] and if you divorce them before consummation, but after the fixation of a dower for them, then the half of dower (is due to them) unless they remit it or I(the man's half) is remitted by him in whose hands is the marriage tie; and the remission (of man's hall) is the nearest to righteousness.[44]

Iddat

o ye who believe When ye marry believing women,
and then divorce them before ye have touched them,
no period of Iddat have you to count in respect of them;
so give them a present,
and set them free in a handsome manner.[45]
O Prophet when ye do divorce women,
divorce them at their prescribed periods
and count (accurately) their presser bed periods .

And turn the not out of their houses
nor shall they leave (themselves) except
in case they are guilty some open lewdness .

Let the women live (in Iddat)
in the same style as ye live,
according to your means,
annoy them not, so as to restrict them.

And ifthey carry (life) them spend (your substance)
on them until they deliver their burden;
and ifthey supple your (off spring) give them
their recompense and take mutual council together,
according to what is just and reasonable.

Khula (Mutual)

If a wife fears cruelty or desertion on her husband part there is no blame on them if they arrange an amicable settlement between themselves and such settlement is best.

Zihar

If any men among you divorce their wives by Zihar (calling them mothers) they can not be their mother, none can be their mothers except those who gave tham birth and in fact, they use words iniquitous and false.

Law relating to Talaq a ordained by Holy Quran is (i) that Talaq must be for reasonable cause, and (ii) that must be preceded by an attempt of reconciliation between husband and wife by the arbitrators, one chosen by the wife from her family and other by the husband from his and in case their attempts fail then Talaq may be effected.

Witness (Revocable and Irrevocable)

Thus, when they fulfill their term appointed, either take them back on equitable terms or part with them on equitable terms and take for witness two persons from among you endued with justice and establish the evidence (as) before God.

Definition of Divorce (Talaq)

The Talaq in its original sense means repudiation or rejection, but under Muslim Law it is a release for the marriage tie either immediately or eventually.[46] The divorce in legal sense means dissolution of marriage tie of husband and wife. According to Muslim Law, a husband, who is of sound mind and has attained puberty, may divorce his wife whenever he desires without assigning any reason, at his mere whim or caprice. Under Shia Law in addition to the requirement of sound mind and puberty free will and intention are essential for valid Talaq. The Talaq, by which is meant dissolution of the marriage in the life time of the parties thereto, may be affected by the act of the husband or by the wife or by mutual agreement; or it may be annulment of the marriage by a decree of a Law Court. Hedaya had defined Talaq as dismissal in the primitive sense.

According to Durrul Mukhtar Talaq signifies "the removal of restraints". But they use the word Talaq in respect of others Talaq (to express the same idea). That is why the expression "Ante Mutlakatun" (which means thou art unrestrained) is held to denote Talaq by implication only. In law it means removal of the restraints of Nikah at one by irrevocable divorce. Legally it would mean dissolution of marriage or the annulment of its legal status by certain words. In fact words Talaq (divorce) and annulment should be considered as separate entities under Muslim Law, because 'Talaq" is only effective by means of a particular word or words while annulment of marriage may be by the exercise of option of emancipation of the option of puberty or by virtue of apostasy. Second group belongs to annulment and not of Talaq. As such the definition given by Kanzud-Dakaik is defective because that definition does not cover case of a reversible divorce. Talaq is the exercise of absolute power of pronouncing unilateral (one sided) divorce on his wife by the husband. Both Shias and Sunnis recognize this husband's authority to pronounce Talaq. The technical meaning of Talaq is freedom from bondage of marriage.[47] This absolute and arbitrary power of Talaq by the husband exists since the Pre-Islamic Period. Ameer Ali[48] remarks that "He (the Prophet) restrained the power of divorce possessed by the husband and towards the end of his life went so far as practically to forbid its exercise the men without the intervention of a Judge."

Similarly, there are many verses in the Quran relating to divorce:

"And if a wife fears ill usage or aversion on the part of her husband, then shall it be no fault if they can agree with mutual agreement, for agreement is best."[49]

"Men are maintainers of women, because Allah has made some of them to excel others and because they spend out of their property (on their maintenance and dower)."

Regarding the recognition of unilateral divorce in Muslim Law, Abdur Rahim says that with a view to regulating the matrimonial relations, predominant position to the husband is allowed. Because generally speaking he is mentally and physically superior of the two: and some theorists would treat that dower payable to the wife as consideration for the alternation of her matrimonial freedom. Technically, the power of the husband to give Talaq is absolute but, virtually and in practice, it is restrained with in definite bounds by the numerous for Mulla which are attached to its exercise.[50] When a man says to his wife "I have divorced thee" either in her presence or in her absence it means that he has divorced her.[51]

The grammatical variations of the word Talaq are terms of arts and have acquired this technical meaning by usage.[52] There are several forms of Talaq sanctioned by the Holy Quran and Hidith. Following are the classification made by the European authors like Juynboll,

(i) By the husband without the intervention of the court.

(ii) By common consent without the intervention of the court.

(iii) By the decree of court on the application of the either party.

But Prof. A.A.A. Fyzee, classified it differently:

(i) By the death of spouse.

(ii) By the Act of the parties.

(iii) By judicial process.

1. Divorce by the Husband

The Talaq in its literal sense this Arabic word means "taking off any tie or restraint" and in law it signifies the dissolution of marriage. In Hanif Law no special form or phrase is necessary to pronounce Talaq. The Ithna Ashari Law, however, insist on strict adherence to a form, that is, it must be in the Arabic language uttered orally, in the presence and hearing of two male witnesses, who should be honest and virtuous Muslims. Even the presence of the wife is not required. The Talaq would be deemed to have taken effect on the date the wife came to know of it.[53] The communication of Talaq becomes necessary in certain cases, as when the wife has to observe Iddat and the dower becomes payable during Iddat. While the Sunnis permit oral and written - both types of Talaq Shias insist on oral Talaq. Any words may be used and it may be given at any time.

In fact, while facing proceedings for maintenance, as for example Under Section 125 Cr.P.C. it is a common practice for the husband to take the plea that he had pronounced Talaq on his wife, and the courts regard it as a conclusive fact of completed divorced. The practice of Talaq almost defies any bondage. The husband holds the key, to assign no reason, to go to no court, take no consent of the wife, give no regard to her condition, follow no procedure or formality, and just pronounce Talaq. How he does it, when he does or in what manner he does it, is not very material.[54] In Hannefa Vs. Pathummal[55] the judicial conscience of Justice Khalid was so much perturbed that he termed the practice as a monstrosity. The Talak-ul-Sunnat is a Talaq which carries the approval of the Prophet Mohammad. It may be in the most approved form of the Talaq in the community of Sunni Muslim.

Talaq-e-Ahsan

Hedaya brands it as the most laudable divorce, where the husband repudiates his wife by a single pronouncement in a period of Tuhr (purity i.e. when the wife is free from her menstrual courses), during which he has not had intercourse with her, and then leaves her to the observance of Iddat. The divorce remains revocable during the Iddat, and the parties retain the right of inheritance.[56] According to the Hedaya, this method of divorce is the most approved because the companions of the Holy Prophet Mohammad approved it, and secondly, because it remains within the power of the husband to revoke the divorce during Iddat, which is three months or ill delivery. In case of a marriage not yet consummated, Ahsan Talaq may be pronounced during menstruation also. Where the wife and husband are living separate from each other, or where the wife is beyond the age of menstruation (in old age), the condition of Tuhr is not applicable, it is also not applicable[57] to a written divorce. This Talaq may be revoked either by express words, or impliedly by cohabitation within the Iddat period. On such revocation, it is not necessary for the wife to undergo intermediary marriage, the husband can simply say "I have retained you". After the Iddat period lapsing without revocation, the Talaq becomes final and irrevocable.

Talaq - e - Hasan

In Talaq Hasan the husband successively pronounces divorce three times during consecutive periods of purity (Tuhr). It is therefore, "a divorce upon a divorce", where the first and second pronouncements are revoked and followed by a third, only then Talaq becomes irrevocable. It is also essential that no intercourse should have taken place during that particular period of purity in which the pronouncement has been made. This may be illustrated thus - When the wife is in Tuhr, without having intercourse with her, the husband pronounces Talaq. Then he revokes it by words or by intercourse, menstruation follows. Again when she is in Tuhr and before intercourse, the husband pronounces Talaq, intercourse follows (repudiation). Again menstruation follows. Now, during Tuhr, without having had intercourse, he pronounces Talaq. This is final and divorce becomes irrevocable. Where the wife is not subject to menstrual courses, an interval of 30 days is required between each successive repudiation.Talaq-e-Hasan tries to put an end to a barbarous Pre-Islamic practice to divorce a wife and take her back several times in order to ill-treat her. Through this method of Talaq, the husband has been given two chances of divorcing and then taking the wife back, but the third time he does so, the Talaq becomes irrevocable. In this way, the process of divorcing and repudiating cannot be continued indefinitely.

Thus it is a kind of relief to the wife from the harassment and tension on account of uncertainty that the Arabs could cause her by repeated Talaq and revocations without limit. The Prophet Mohammad restrained them to the limit of three repetitions. Further shackle on the overbearing males was by way of the requirements of intermediary marriage, its consummation and divorce before remarriage with such wife. Of course the aspect of her further humiliation involved in this process was overlooked.

Talak-ul-Biddat

The husband does not follow the approved form of Talaq that is Talaq-ul-Sunnat and neither pays any attention to the period of purity nor to the abstention from intercourse. This was an escape lane from the restrictions imposed by the Prophet Mohammad, as just above. As Ameer Ali observed that the Omayyad monarchs finding that the check imposed by the Prophet Mohammad on the facility of repudiation interfered with the indulgence of their caprice, endeavored to find an escape from the strictness of law and found a loophole to effect their purpose.[58]

Triple Divorce

Hedaya defines it as a divorce where the husband repudiates his wife by three divorces in one sentence, or where he repeats the sentence, separately, thrice within Tuhr. Such a divorce is lawful, although sinful, in Hanafi Law; but in Shia Law it is not permissible.[59] Thus he may pronounce 'I divorce you, 1 divorce you, 1 divorce you; this is triple divorce or he may say 'I divorce you thrice'. Even the triple form is not an indispensable requirement. He may say 'I divorce you in Talaq-ulBiddat or Talaq-ul-Bain form. Where the intention is clear the divorce is irrevocable.

None of these forms is recognized by Shias. After such divorce also, like in Hasan Talaq, intermediary marriage is necessary for reunion. This condemned form is considered heretical because of its irrevocability. Talaq-ul-Biddat is good in law though bad in theology, and is most commonly practiced in India. The courts have refused to derecognize it.[60]

One Irrevocable Divorce

The husband may say that he divorces his wife a hundred times, the Talaq is complete. So also if he shows his intention in writing, for example he writes "I by my free will divorce my wife by one Talaq-ul-Bain (irrevocable divorce) and renounce her from the state of being my wife," an irrevocable divorce has been effect.

Talaq

When Talaq becomes irrevocable:

(i) Talaq-ul-Ashan becomes irrevocable on the completion of the period of Iddat.

(ii) Talaq-ul-Hasan comes into force on the very point when the third pronouncement is made. The factor of Iddat has no influence on it.

(iii) Talaq-ul-Biddat of both types triple or single also becomes irrevocable right on pronouncement

(iv) In case of unconsummated marriage Talaq becomes irrevocable right on pronouncement.

(v) A written Talaq comes into effect from the moment of its execution, unless it is ambiguous.[61]

Effect of Compulsion, Intoxication or Jest

Hanafi Jurists consider a Talaq given by a man under compulsion is valid, while Imam Shafii, Malik and Hanbal and Shia Jurists consider it as invalid. Divorce given under the influence of intoxication is valid according to Hanafi Law, whereas Shias do not recognize it. Hanafi Jurists hold that when a husband becomes intoxicated of his own free will, and repudiates his wife, the divorce is valid, but if he was intoxicated under a compulsion or from necessity, there is no divorce. Hanafi Law, as distinguished from the Shia Law, holds a divorce pronounced in jest (joke, fun, non seriously) as valid.

Ila (Vow of continence)

An Ila is when a person swears that he will not have sexual intercourse with his wife and abstains from it for four months, the divorce is effected. The Hanafi Jurists argue that since the husband acted unjustly towards his wife, it is equitable that on the expiation of four months he should be deprived of the benefit of marriage. The Shafiis and Shias consider that such a vow does not amount to divorced. but only gives the wife a ground to seek judicial divorce. In Sunni Law legal proceeding are not required. The intent of the husband must to express clearly. In Rahema Khatoon V s. Iqtidar-ud-din[62] the husband, on entering the room of the wife on the very first day of the marriage called her 'a wife in name only'. The Court refused to accept it as an Ila in absence of a clear intention. According to Asharis this form of divorce can be given when then marriage has been consummated. The Hanafi Law provides that an Ila can be retracted by resumption of cohabitation or even by verbal retraction if actual cohabitation is not possible due to some reasons. Even after the expiry of four months the husband can cancel to divorce of Ila with the assent of the wife. At present this form of Talaq is not in practice in India.

2. By the Wife - Talaq-e- Tafwid (delegated divorce)

This doctrine is peculiar to the Muslim Law and has no parallel in other systems. That is the husband may delegate the powers of divorce to his wife. He may do so at the time of marriage contract or at any time when he so likes. Baillie defines it that "as a man may in person repudiates his wife, so he may commit the power of repudiating her to herself or to a third party. A.A.A.Fyzee says that this form of delegated divorce is now beginning to be fairly common in India. The Indian High Courts have repeatedly held as valid the agreement by which the husband authorizes the wife to divorce herself from him in the event of his marrying a second wife without her consent. There are three forms of Tafwid. The delegation must be made in clear terms and circumstances in which the wife (or a minor wife's guardian) is to exercise the choice must be spelt clearly. The conditions must not be opposed to public policy. Thus delegation of the right to Talaq in case the husband fails to pay her maintenance may be delegated.[63] The wife must exercise her option expressly; mere happening of the stipulated event would not per se result in Talaq.[64] The power may be delegated at the time of nuptial agreement or during the married life. The power so delegated cannot be revoked by the husband. The wife may exercise the power to counter a suit for restitution of conjugal rights instituted by the husband, and such exercise will be called a divorce of wife by husband, as she would be acting on his behalf. In spite of such delegation the husband retains the right to Talaq her according to his choice.

3. By Mutual Consent. - (i) Khula (redemption)

If the mutual relationship between the husband and wife is not good, the wife, if so she desires, may seek a Khula divorce i.e. by relinquishing her claim to the dower. It however, entirely depends upon the husband to accept the consideration of dower and to grant the divorce. A husband may similarly propose a Khula divorce; the wife may accept or refuse it. If she accepts, it means that she has relinquished the right to get dower from her husband. Khula may be for any consideration i.e. dower, money, property, etc. The wife's failure to pay the consideration agreed upon in a Khula divorce does not invalidate the divorce, so as to enable the husband to sue for restitution of conjugal rights, but only entitles him (a) to claim the release of dower, or (b) to sue for any money or property due under the agreement. In the leading case on Khula divorce is Moonshee Buz-ul-Raheem Vs. Lateefa-un-Nissa,[65] in which it was observed that a divorce by Khula is at once complete from the moment when the husband repudiates the wife. There is no period during which such a divorce can be repudiated.

Mulla considers Khula as a divorce by mutual consent; but Paras Diwan differs, saying that since in Khula the desire to separate emanates from the wife, and she has to make her husband agree to it by offering consideration, it would be proper to call it divorce at the instance of the wife.[66] Both husband and wife must be of sound mind and have attained puberty. Hanafis and Shafiis permit the guardian of the minor wife to enter into Khula on her behalf; but not the guardian of the minor husband. Shias insist that there must be no compulsion exerted on the mind of the wife, while Sunnis would not mind Khula obtained under compulsion. Sunnis also recognize a conditional Khula; not so the Shias. Hanafi Law permits the wife to retain an option to revoke the Khula. If the husband stipulates such an option, the Khula will be deemed irrevocable and the option void. Under Shia Law, both the Khula and the option would be void; for the Khula must be unconditional. All schools agree, in Khula the consent of the husband in clear words is a must. The wife may revoke the Khula before the agreement is finalized by getting up from the meeting. Hanafi regard Khula as a Talaq-ul-Bain, an irrevocable divorce. Shia

Jurists differ on the point whether wife and husband can remarry immediately after Khula. Ithna Asharis hold it irrevocable, but the husband may revoke the Khula.

(ii) Mubara'at (mutual freeing)

When the divorce is affected by mutual consent of the husband and wife, it is known as Mubara'at (i.e. freeing one another mutually). It has been held in a Pakistani case,[67] that such matters as "incompatibility of temperaments, aversion or dislike cannot from a ground for a wife to seek dissolution of her marriage, at the hands of a Qazi or a Court but they fall to be dealt with under the powers possessed by the husband as well as the wife under Muslim Law" that is, the capacity of making a Khula or Mubara'at divorce. Khula and Mubara'at are irrevocable divorce; Iddat become necessary for wife, and she is entitled to maintenance.

The word Mubara'a or Mubara'at indicates the freeing of each other (from the marriage tie) by mutual agreement. As A.A.A.Fyzee[68] puts it, while in Khula the request proceeds from the wife to be released and the husband agrees for certain consideration, usually the Mahr, in Mubara'at apparently both are happy at the prospects of being rid of each other. No formal form is insisted upon for Mubara'at by the Sunnis. The offer may come from either side. When both the parties enter into Mubara'at all mutual rights and obligations come to an end. Both Shia and Sunni Laws hold it an irrevocable divorce. The Iddat is compulsory after Mubara'a at as after Khula.

By Judicial Process - (i) Lian (Mutual Imprecation)

The wife is entitled to sue for a divorce on the ground that her husband has falsely charged with adultery. At the hearing of the suit, the husband had two alternatives;

(i) he may retract (withdraw) the charge before the end of the trial, in which case the wife could not get a divorce, or

(ii) to persist in his attitude, whereby her will be required to accuse is wife on oath.

This is followed by oaths of innocence made by the wife. After these "mutual imprecations" and the court dissolves the marriage. The husband and wife both must be sane adults; the charge must be false, i.e. one not proved to be true; the wife must tile a regular suit for the dissolution of marriage making the false charge the ground for seeking divorce. Mere lying of charge by husband or mere application to the court complaining that the husband had falsely charged her of adultery would not by itself amount to divorce. Their marriage must be Sahih and not Fasid. When dissolved by the court, it would be an irrevocable consequence. The doctrine of Lian is still accepted by courts as a valid Muslim Law procedure. In Nurjahan Bibi Vs. Mohd. Kazim Ali[69] whereon husband bringing a false charge on wife (Lian) the court granted the wife the decree for dissolution of marriage Under Section 2 (ix) of the Dissolution of Muslim Marriages Act, 1939, it was observed by Justice Bhattacharaya that the doctrine of Lian had not become obsolete. The practice is based on tradition. Husband and wife both have to take oath inviting God's curse on liar. If the husband's charge is proved, the wife loses the ground for dissolution. If he fails, she can get the divorce as well as sue the husband for defamation under the Indian Penal Code for bringing a false charge of adultery amounts to cruelty against the wife and attracts the Section 2 (viii) of the Act, 1939 and the Exception-I Under Section.499 I.P.C would not apply.[70] In a Lian suit the burden of proof lies on the wife. According to Malik[71] this holding is against Muslim Law where it is provided that the husband must prove the charge of adultery or suffer the consequences.

Retraction of Charge

There are two conflicting stands among the courts about retraction of charge by the husband. In Tufail Ahmad Vs. Jamila Khatun[72] the Allahabad High Court held that retraction of charge by husband before the wife brought the suit for dissolution of marriage on the ground of false charge was sufficient to dismiss the wife's suit. The retraction must be honest and genuine, not malafide to defeat the suit. He must acknowledge that he had falsely accused her, and he must be punished for this. In such a retraction though he may be held liable for slander or defamation, the marriage cannot be dissolved. The Calcutta High Court[73] allowed retraction at any time before the close of the evidence. The Bombay High Court[74] had held on the other hand that retraction had no place in the procedure of Indian courts, but later the Court had retracted from this holding.[75] In an earlier decision the Allahabad High Court had also held that after the passing of the 1939 Act, there was not place for retraction under the Act, and it amounted to cruelty by the husband.[76] The commenting on Lian form

B.N.Sampath scholar has observed that It is interesting to note the difference in approach of the modern systems and the Islamic law. Whereas an unsubstantiated charge of adultery is of no consequence under most of the modern laws, in Islamic Law it leads to divorce. On the contrary, while proven adultery leads to divorce under most of the modern systems, it does not, under the Islamic law of Lian ; however, proved adultery will lead to death of the wife under the Islamic Criminal Law. Since Islamic Criminal Law has no validity in India, its corresponding limb the Lian, may also be given up.

(ii) Faskh (Judicial Annulment)

The Faskh means annulment. It refers to the power of Qazi (in India) to annual a marriage on the application of the wife. The law of Faskh is founded upon Quran and Traditions, "If a woman be prejudiced by a marriage, let it be broken off' (Bokhari). In India, such judicial annulments are governed by Under Section 2 of the Dissolution of Muslim Marriages Act, 1939. Prior to the Act, the Muslim woman could apply for dissolution of marriage under the doctrine of Faskh on four grounds :

(i) The marriage was irregular,
(ii) In exercise of the right of opinion (Khyar-ul-Bulugh),
(iii) The marriage was within the prohibited degrees of relationship,
(iv) Post-marriage of the parties to the Islam.[77]

Two more grounds could be added: Impotency of the husband and Lian. In K.C.Moyin Vs. Nafeesa[78] the court had held that under no circumstances could a Muslim woman unilaterally repudiate a marriage by Faskh, it had no legal sanction without seeking the intervention of the court. Prior to this Act, the classical Hanafi Law of divorce was causing hardships as it consisted no provision whereby a Hanafi wife could seek divorce on such grounds as disappearance of the husband, his long imprisonment, his neglect of matrimonial obligations etc. Finding no other way to get rid of undesired marital bonds, many Muslim women felt compelled by their circumstances to renounce their faith. The Statement of the Reasons and Objects of this Act indicates the circumstances in which this Act was passed:

"There is no provisions in the Hanafi Code of Muslim Law enabling a married Muslim woman to obtain a decree from the courts dissolving her marriage in case the husband neglects to maintain her, makes her life miserable by deserting or persistently ill-treating her or certain other circumstances. The absence of such a provision has entailed unspeakable misery to innumerable Muslim women in British India, the Hanaji Jurists, however, have clearly laid down that in cases in which the application of Hanaji Law causes hardship, it is permissible to apply the provision of the Maliki, Shafii or Hanbali Law. Acting on this principle the Ulema have issued Fatawas to the effect that in cases enumerated in Clause 3, Part A of this Bill, a married Muslim woman may obtain a decree dissolving her marriage. A lucid exposition of this principle can be found in the book called Heelat-un-Najeza published by Maulana Ashraf Ali Sahib (Thanvi) who has made an exhaustive study of the provisions of Maliki Law which under the circumstances prevailing in India may be applied to such cases, this has been approved by a large number of Ulema who put their seals of approval on the book."

"As the courts are sure to hesitate to apply the Maliki Law to the case of a Muslim woman, legislation recognizing and enforcing the above-mentioned principle is called for in order to relieve the sufferings of countless Muslim women."

In view of the above reasons, the Dissolution of Muslim Marriages Act,1939 was passed. It is applicable to all Muslims in India who may otherwise adhere to Hanafi, Shafii, Ithna Ashari or Ismaili Law. The Act is in force throughout India except in the State of Jammu and Kashmir, where a parallel enactment by the name of Jammu and Kashmir State Dissolution of Muslim Marriages Act, 1942 is in force. The words used by Section 2 of the Act are a "woman married under Muslim Law", and not a 'Muslim woman'. This protects women who have already abjured Islam in the hope of getting their marriage dissolved and are thus no longer Muslims; they also can get their marriage dissolved on any of the grounds given in the Act. The Act consolidates and clarifies the Muslim Law relating to suits for dissolution of marriage by women. It is applicable to all Muslims but the provisions of this Act have to be applied by taking recourse to ordinary process of the civil courts of the country. An appeal against order of the subordinate court is competent Under Section 96 of the Code of Civil Procedure. Section 2 of the Act lays down the grounds on which a Muslim woman can seek divorce.

Grounds for decree for Dissolution of Marriage

A woman married under Muslim Law shall be entitled to obtain a decree for the dissolution of her marriage on anyone: or more of the following grounds, namely:

(i) that the whereabouts of the husband have not been known for a period of four years;

(ii) that the husband has neglected or has failed to provide for her maintenance for a period of two years;

(iii) that the husband has been sentenced to imprisonment for a period of seven years or upwards;

(iv) that the husband has failed to perform, without reasonable cause, his marital obligations for a period of three years;

(v) that the husband was impotent at the time of the marriage and continues to be so ;

(vi) that the husband has been insane for a period of two years or is suffering from leprosy or a virulent venereal disease;

(vii) that she, having been given in marriage by her father or other guardian before she attained the age of fifteen years, repudiated the marriage before attaining the age of eighteen years;

(viii) that the husband treats her with cruelty that is to say.

(a) habitually assaults her or makes her life miserable by cruelty of conduct even if such conduct does not amount to physical ill-treatment, or

(b) associates with women of evil repute or leads an infamous life, or

(c) attempts to force her to lead an immoral life, or

(d) disposes of her property or prevents her exercising her legal rights over it, or

(e) obstructs her in the observance of her religious profession or practice, or

(f) if he has more wives than one, does not treat her equitably in accordance with the injunctions of the Quran.

(ix) on any other ground which is recognized as valid for the Talaq/ dissolution of marriages under Muslim Law provided that:

(a) no decree shall be passed on ground (iii) until the sentence has become final;

(b) a decree passed on ground (i) shall not take effect for period of six months from the date of such decree and if the husband appears either in person or through an authorized agent within that period and satisfies the court that he is prepared to perform his conjugal duties, the court shall set aside the said decree; and

(c) before passing a decree on ground (v) the court shall, on application by the husband, make an order requiring the husband to satisfy the court within a period of one year from the date of such order that he has ceased to be impotent and if the husband so satisfies the court within such period, no decree shall be passed on the said ground.

Iddat : Rationale, Utility and Periods

Iddat its importance - Hedaya defines it as " the term of probation incumbent upon a woman in consequence of the dissolution of marriage after carnal connection." It has been further said in Hedaya that "that most approved definition of Iddat is, the term by the completion of which a new marriage is rendered lawful".

Thus, Iddat is the period for which a woman must wait before marrying again whether in the event of divorce or death. The different periods of Iddat are as follows:

Cause of dissolution	**Marriage whether consummated or not**	**Period of Iddat**
Divorce	Consummated	3 Courses or, if pregnant, till delivery
Divorce	Not consummated	No Iddat
Death	Does't matter	4 Months &10 days or, if pregnant, till delivery whichever period is longer.

In certain cases, 'Valid Retirement' has the same legal effect as consummation. When the husband and wife are alone together under circumstances, which present no legal, moral or physical impediment to marital intercourse, they are said to be in valid retirement. Thus the period of Iddat prescribed in case of consummation will apply in case of 'valid retirement' also.

The reason for observing Iddat in the case of divorce are:

(i) to ascertain whether the woman is pregnant, and

(ii) to provide an opportunity to the husband to take the wife back (in revocable forms of Talaq)

And in case of death, the Iddat is :

(i) to ascertain whether the woman is pregnant, and

(ii) to provide a period of mourning for the deceased husband.

The period of 4 months and 10 days has been fixed with a view that in such a time pregnancy would become perceptible; if it does not, the Iddat is terminated. If pregnancy appears, Iddat continues till delivery. The period of 4 months and 10 days has also been considered by Muslim Jurists as sufficient period of mourning. Similarly, in case of divorce, the period of Iddat is three courses, because, it has been felt by jurists that one or two menstruation courses, because, it has been felt by jurists that one or two menstruation courses may not be sufficient to ascertain pregnancy. If the divorced woman is not of age as to be menstruating, then her Iddat lasts for three months, since most women menstruate monthly and a month is equal to one menstrual period. It is one of the legal fictions of Muslim Law that a marriage is taken to subsist even after it is dissolved, notwithstanding that the husband has died or pronounced a divorce. This legal fiction affects the woman's rights in the following matters, namely (i) remarriage, (ii) her maintenance (iii) right to inherit from her husband, (iv) prohibition against unlawful conjunction (that is husband's remarriage with her sister). The woman undergoing Iddat is also expected to observe Hidad, that is, abstinence from things of luxury. But according to Shias and Shafiis, it is not necessary. Since no legal consequences flow out of nonobservance of

Hidad it carries only moral force. The wife is also expected to remain where she was at the time of death or divorce. But this prohibition is also not followed nowadays.

Under Shia Law, if a man knows that the woman he is marrying is under an obligation to observe Iddat, then the marriage would be void. In case such a marriage is consummated, the parties are perpetually debarred from intermarrying. In the absence of consummation, however, marriage is possible after the woman has completed her Iddat. The Shia Law also provides that an old woman who can now no more become pregnant, or is so young as to be below the age of puberty, need not observe Iddat. The woman must observe the prescribed period of Iddat when a Muta marriage is dissolved by death or divorce. If husband dies during Iddat, Hanafi Law says, a fresh Iddat becomes necessary. The period of this Iddat, in the view of Imam Mohammad and Abu Handa, is three menstrual courses, provided the divorce is pronounced in an irrevocable form. If the woman is not having courses., the fresh Iddat has to be prolonged so as to include them. Abu Yusuf, however, says that it is only three courses, without any prolongation.

Effects of Divorce

(i) Cohabitation becomes illegal between the couple.

(ii) Dower becomes payable to the wife. But Mohd. Ahmed Khan Vs. Shah Bano Begum[79] it has been laid down that dower is not payable on divorce but is payable on marriage.

(iii) The husband and the wife are entitled to inherit from other, if either of them dies during Iddat following a revocable divorce. No right of inheritance arises in irrevocable divorce.

(iv) The wife becomes entitled to maintenance during the period of Iddat.

(v) Remarriage between the couple is only possible after observing a strict procedure. Remarriage with another man can be contracted by the widow after observing Iddat only.

Formalities necessary for Re-Marriage

Where the husband has divorced his wife by three pronouncements (irrevocable divorce) remarriage with her is possible only if the following formalities are observed:

(i) After the divorce, the wife should observe Iddat.

(ii) When the period of Iddat expires, she should marry another person.

(iii) This marriage should be actually consummated.

(iv) The second husband should voluntarily divorce the wife.

(v) Then the wife should observe Iddat, after which remarriage with ex-husband would be possible. If remarriage takes place without fulfilling the above requirements, it is irregular but not void.

In the leading case of Rashid Ahmad Vs. Anisa Khatun[80] it was held by the Privy Council that where a husband irrevocably divorced his wife but continued to live together as husband and wife, then the children of such a union would be illegitimate; even an acknowledgment of legitimacy could not make them legitimate. It must be noted here that not only the necessary formalities were evaded in this case, but even a remarriage was not formally contracted, otherwise, such a marriage being irregular (and not void), the children would have been legitimate.

Islamic Reforms and Triple Talaq

According to Ameer Ali the Prophet of Islam is reported to have said with Allah, the most detestable of all thing permitted is divorce, and towards he the end of his life he practically for bade its exercise by men without intervention of an arbiter or a judge. The Quran ordains....

"If ye fear a breach between them twain (the husband and the wife) appoint an arbiter from his folk. If they desire amendment, Allah will make them of one mind. "

The Quran permit is partly because of some countenance to the customs and partly to enable men to get rid of an odious union. The Prophet Mohammad restrained the power of divorce and gave to the woman the right of obtaining separation on reasonable grounds. The Prophet Mohammad is reported to have said, "If a woman be prejudiced by a marriage, let it be broken off". Almost all the doctrines of Muslim Law hold Talaq permitted though they regard its exercise without any cause morally and religiously abominable. They quote the Prophet Mohammad as saying "that curse of God rests on him who repudiates his wife capriciously."

Generally, both the parties to the marriage contract have an option for divorce, but the husband's right in this respect is much greater than that of the wife. The husband can dissolve the marriage tie at his will. A divorce can also take place by mutual agreement. But the wife cannot divorce herself from her husband without his consent.

She can of course purchase her divorce from her husband and can have the marriage dissolved by Tafwid (delegation). In a case of Assam High Court, Zeenat Fatima Vs. Modh. Iqbal Anwar- the petitioner Zeenat married Iqbat in 1987. They had a son in 1989 and that she was ill-treated by her husband and in-laws. She instituted a criminal case. She had to leave her husband's house. She instituted to leave her husband's house. She instituted a criminal case for getting back her properties which were recovered. She also filed a case Under Section 125 of the Criminal Procedure Code against her husband claiming maintenance for herself and her minor child and Iqbal contested the case by filing written statement. His main defense is that he had divorced his wife in 1990. The family court held that there had been a divorce duly affected and therefore, claim for maintenance would be determined U/s. of Muslim Woman (Protection of Rights on Divorce) Act, 1986. Interim maintenance for the child was granted pending final disposal of the case. Hence in this petition, the question which arises for consideration is whether there had been a divorce duly effected.

Under the Quran, the marriage state is to be maintained as far as possible and there should be conciliation before divorce.[81] Therefore, a Mohammedan husband cannot divorce his wife at his whim and caprice. The question then is whether, if divorce by Talaq is made arbitrarily, should it be treated as spiritual offence only? Under the Muslim Law, marriage though regarded as a civil contract between a man and a woman; they become husband and wife after solemnization of the marriage and their respective rights and obligations are regulated by the rules under relevant law. This being the position, marriage is the basis for social organization and foundation of legal rights and obligations. The modern concept of divorce is also that the matrimonial status should be maintained as far as possible. The Family Court aims at reconciliation and persuasion of parties to arrive at a settlement. For these reasons if a Muslim husband divorces his wife at his whim and caprice, it would not only be a spiritual offence but it would also affect the divorce. In the above view of the matter, a Mohammedan husband cannot divorce his at his whim or caprice, that is, divorce must be for a reasonable cause, and it must be preceded by a pre-divorce conference to arrive at a settlement. The case is solely based on Talaqnama which has not been proved, and there was no evidence that there was a pre-divorce conference. In that view of the matter the husband has failed to prove the alleged divorce by Talaq.

Triple Talaq

According to Ashgar Ali Engineer the Islamic Shariah which was formulated more than hundred years after the death of the Holy Prophet Mohammad and had evolved under complex influences of various civilizations took away what was given to women by the Prophet Mohammad and the Quran. The issue of triple divorce in one sitting illustrates this every well. It was practiced during Jahilliyah period (times of ignorance) before the advent of the Islam. The usual practice then was to pronounce the word Talaq two times and withhold the third pronouncement, making the wife live thus in constant fear of the third utterance.

The triple divorce was not all allowed during the Prophet Mohammad's lifetime, during the first Caliph Abu Bakr's reign and also for more than two years during the second Calipha Umar's time. Later on Calipha Umar permitted it on account a peculiar situation. When the Arabs conquered Syria, Egypt, Persia etc. they found women there much more beautiful than their own women and hence were tempted to marry them. But those women not knowing about Islam's abolition of triple divorce in one sitting, would insist that before marrying them they should pronounce divorce thrice to their existing wives which they would readily accept to do (as they knew the Islam had abolished triple divorce and that it would not be effective) and marry the Syrian or Egyptian women and would also retain their earlier wives. When the Egyptian and Syrian women discovered that they had been cheated, they complained to Calipha Umar. The Caliph then enforced triple divorce again in order to prevent its misuse by the Arabs. He had done so to meet an emergency situation and not to enforce irs permanently. But later jurists also declared this form of divorce valid and gave sanction to it. The Hadiath literature records that when the Prophet Mohammad was told that so and so had divorced his wife thrice in one sitting his face turned red with anger and he stood up and said he was ridiculing the divine law in the Prophet Mohammad's own life time and required that the man took back his wife. The Quran does not mention triple divorce in one sitting. It requires the divorce to be effective over three periods of cleanliness, giving the couple a chance to reconcile during those three months. The Quran also provides for arbitration both to men and women appointing arbiter for each and they together would attempt reconciliation failing which the decision for divorce will be recommended to Qazi. Thus, both the Quran and the Prophet Mohammad prohibit arbitrary divorce. All precautions were taken to guard woman's interests. However the later jurists intluenced by the male dominated values of the patriarchal society gave man absolute right to divorce his wife and brought back a measure which was Pre-Islamic and which was strongly condemned by the Prophet Mohammad. A Fatwa given by a Mufti of Ahl-e-Hadith rejecting the validity of triple divorce brought the Talaq issue to focus again. Maulana Asad Madani, President of the powerful Jamiate-Ulema-e-Hind has strongly opposed the Fatwa and declared it void in the Islamic and a conspiracy against the spouses in concern. The progressive Muslim intellectuals like Maulana Wahiduddin Khan and Engineer have upheld the Fatwa. They argue that if the Shariah is truly based on the Quran and Sunnah then there is no place for the pronouncement of triple divorce in one sitting. Imam-Ibn- Taimiyyah, a jurist of the 14thCentury and his disciple Ibn-Qayyim-Jawzi had also held the triple divorce in one sitting invalid. All the Ulemas also agree that this divorce is Bidah (innovation) and hence sinful. It is also unjust to the Muslim women. Ashgar Ali Engineer feels that it is high time the Muslim Personal Law Board recommended a Bill to the Government abolishing the triple Talaq in one sitting and enforcing the Quranic form of divorce which is very far to woman.

In Aziza Khan Vs. Dr. Amir Hussain the petitioner was married with the respondent in 1982 in accordance with the Muslim rites and customs and Rs.10,000 were settled as the Mahr amount in case of Talaq The petitioner was an advocate and the non-petitioner was a doctor. The petitioner's case was that the non-petitioner was having illicit relations with two ladies and she herself was subjected to in-human treatment. It was alleged that the doctor was not satisfied with the dowry given by her parents and she was asked to fetch more money from her father who was a Minister at that time. The respondent denied all charges and asserted that he had given her Talaq by written Talaqnama in 1986 and addressed it to her by registered post. He refuted responsibility to pay her maintenance after passing of the Muslim Women Act, 1986. The point of central importance for us here is the argument of the petitioner that the Talaq was not valid on account of two lacunae, one, there was no attempt for reconciliation, and two, pre-divorce conference was not held. Both these arguments were contested by the respondent pointing out that the provision in the Quran for an attempt of settlement or pre-divorce conference were directory in nature and their non-compliance did not render the Talaq invalid. The High Court held that both the grounds were not mandatory according to the Quran and there was no authority that in their absence the Talaq was rendered invalid. In Koushar Ali Laskar Vs. Moslema Bibi[82] , the husband petitioner could not pay his wife the maintenance. She refused to live with him because of his T.B. So he pronounced Talaq in accordance with Muslim rites and custom, and filed an application Under Section 127 of the Criminal Procedure Code for quashing of the maintenance order. The wife contested the factum of the proof of the divorce. The High Court found that the Talaqnama was reduced into writing by the Chief Imam of a mosque in the presence of witnesses and the same communicated to the wife after eight months. The High Court held that the Talaq was duly proved and valid. Thus, it can be seen that in the matter of procedure of Talaq, including its testimony, timing, instruments, retrospective effect & etc the courts considered the husband's authority as almost undisputable. Is this kind of arbitrariness religiously sanctioned in Muslim Law?

In this context, Justice S.A.Kader[83] has rightly stated that According to Moulana Mohamed Ali the practice in those early the Islamic days was for the Qazi to appoint two arbitrators one from the husband's family and the other from the wife's family, that those two arbitrators have to try to effect a reconciliation between the parties and if all hopes of reconciliation fail, a divorce is allowed, but the final decision for divorce rests with the Qazi, who is legally entitled to pronounce divorce. This is a procedure par excellence, which portrays Islam in its true glory. But later Muslim Jurists of 'great antiquity and high authority; threw to the winds this salutary procedure and conceived or rather misconceived a form under which a husband can bring about dissolution of marriage by unilateral pronouncement of

Talaq thrice in one sitting called Talaq-ul-Biddat or Talaq-i-Badi which is not recognized in the Holy Book."

Further Justice Kader quotes Ameer Ali citing an incident that "As a matter of fact, the capricious and irregular exercise of power of divorce which was in the beginning left to the husbands was strongly disapproved by the Prophet Mohammad. It is reported that when once news was brought to him that one of his disciples had divorced his wife pronouncing the three Talaqs at one and at the same time, the Prophet Mohammed stood up in anger on his carpet and declared that the man was making a play thing of the words of God and made him take back his wife."

Now the Supreme Court has derecognized the husband's dicat to divorce in any manner, from any date past of future and without any proof. The Apex Court held in Shamim Ara Vs. State of U.P.[84], that the condition precedent for effectiveness of divorce was the pronouncement of divorce which has to be proved on evidence. Merely taking a plea in the written statement before the trial court in reply to an application for maintenance, that the husband had divorced the applicant sometime in the past would not have the effect of effectuating a divorce. Nor could a similar statement made in an affidavit by the husband in some other case to which the wife was not even a party, be regarded as an evidence of divorce accomplished.

The appellant herein as S and the non-appellant (one Abrar Ahmed, referred as A or husband) were married in 1968. In 1979 S filed an application Under Section 125 of the Criminal Procedure Code. In 1979, complaining of cruelty to her and her children as well as desertion. A replied by claiming divorce, done in 11.7.1987, therefore her dis entitlement for maintenance. No statement of circumstances, no justification by reasons, no proof of efforts of reconciliation and no evidence of witnesses in support of the Talaq were adduced. The family Court had accepted an affidavit by A in some case where S was not even a party as a proof of the Talaq. The High Court of Allahabad held that although the alleged divorce had not been communicated to the appellant S that stood completed in 1990 when the husband filed written statement to her appeal.

In this appeal by special leave the Supreme Court observed:

"None of the ancient Holy Books or scriptures of Muslims mentions such a form of divorce........a recital in any document, whether a pleading or an affidavit incorporating a statement by the husband that he has already divorced his wife on an unspecified or specified date even if not communicated to the wife would become an effective divorce on the date on which the wife happens to learn of such statement ...."

The Supreme Court noted the views of Mulla (Mulla on Principles of Mohammedan Law, 19th Edn., 1990) that no particular form of words, no proof of intention, no presence of wife, no communication except for the purposes of dower were required: and to Tahir Mahmood (The Muslim Law of India, 21 nd Edn.) That the basic rule is that a Muslim husband under all schools of Muslim Law can divorce his wife by his unilateral action and without the intervention of the court. Both have cited cases supporting their views. The Supreme Court expressed disapproval and disagreement with the above views. The approving the decisions of Gauhati High Court in Jai-ud-din Ahmed Vs. Anwara Begum[85], and Rukia Khatun Vs. Abdul Khalik Laskar[86], by the Apex Court of India held:

"The correct law of Talaq as ordained by the Holy Quran is that Talaq must be for a reasonable cause and be preceded by attempts at reconciliation between the husband and the wife by two arbitrators- one from the wife's family and the other from the husband's: if the attempts fail, Talaq may be effected. .... We are also of the opinion that the Talaq to be effective has to be pronounced. We are very clear that a mere plea taken in the written statement of a divorce having been pronounced sometime in the past cannot by itself be treated as effectuating Talaq on the date of delivery of the copy of the written statement to the wife. The husband ought to adduce evidence and prove the pronouncement of Talaq ...."[87]

This judgment can be expected to restrain the Muslim husbands from playing the trump card of divorce to defeat the wife's demand for maintenance. Now he will have to prove reconciliation efforts, establish reasonable grounds, and show two witnesses, in whose presence Talaq was pronounced. The wife's side being involved (in the reconciliation efforts) it is not so easy now to 'manage' all this Further, requirements of consent by the wife and dated receipt of the Talaqnama,or, alternatively order of the Court (accepting the reasonableness of the Talaq by the husband) may prove as effective check on the misuse of the power. The further requirement of 'reasonable provision' ordered by the Supreme Court in Danial Latifi's case makes the wife's position better guarded than before. In essence, it is a matter of attitude: attitude towards the wife, towards the relationship, towards the family. It is one of those areas of Muslim Law where reform is overdue. The very idea of unilateral divorce militates against the real spirit behind Islamic Law of marriage and divorce. Divorce is permissible in the Islam only in cases of extreme emergency when all efforts at reconciliation have failed. But unfortunately, " it is the Islamic Law of divorce not polygamy which is the major cause of suffering to Muslim women the Muslim wife indeed has always lived, so far as the law is concerned" under the ever present shadow of divorce"

We know that there are two types of Talaq i.e. Talaq-ul-Sunnat and Talaq-ul-Biddat: the former is approved while the latter is disapproved in the Islam. Talaq-ul-Biddat came into being during the second century of Islam when "the Omayyad monarchs, finding that the checks imposed by the Prophet Mohammed on the facility of repudiation interfered with the indulgence of their caprice, endeavored to find and escape from the strictness of the law, and found ....a loophole to effect their purposes."[88]

It must be noted clearly that it was not Islam but Omayyad practices that gave validity to these 'Biddat' divorces. It has recently been pointed out by Justice Iyyer in Abdul Yusuf Vs. Sowramma[89] where he said that:

"It is a popular fallacy that a Muslim male enjoys under the Quranic Law, unbridled authority to liquidate the marriage the view that the Muslim husband enjoys an arbitrary, unilateral power to inflict divorce does not accord with Islamic injunctions. However,

Muslim Law, as applied in India, has taken a course contrary to the spirit of what the Prophet Mohammed or the Holy Quran laid down and the same misconception vitiates the law dealing with the wife's right to divorce............... Commentators on the Quran have rightly observed and this tallies with the law now administered in some Muslim countries like Iraq - that the husband must satisfy the court about the reasons for divorce"

Talaq-ul-Biddat should, therefore, be not given effect to Fyzee denounces such Talaqs as "absurd and unjust", and suggests that the proper remedy is to do away with them by statute. Ameer Ali suggest that Shafit Law be made applicable to Muslims in India. Abdur Rahim is more pungent when he says"

" I may remark that the interpretation of law of divorce by the jurists specially of the Hanif School, is one flagrant instance where because of literal adherence to mere words and a certain tendency towards subtleties they have reached a result in direct antagonism to the admitted policy of the law on the subject.........."[90]

Far reaching reforms relating to unilateral divorce have been introduced during the recent years, in a large number of Muslim countries[91]. According to Kadar, in Algeria, Tunisia, Turkey, South Yemen, Malasia and Indonesia the practice of extra-judicial unilateral divorce has been abolished. Algerian Family Code, 1984 requires attempt of reconciliation and judgment of the Quadi. In Turkey divorce is recognized only when granted by the Court. The court's decree also provides for maintenance, residence, custody of the children and compensation. Yemen Family Law, 1974 also requires approval of the District Court after satisfactory efforts for reconciliation. Malaysian Islamic Family Law, 1984 punishes a man for divorcing his wife outside the court, and divorce is permissible only after judicial investigation into causes of the breakdown. Indonesia also adopts similar policy. In Egypt, Jordan, Morocco, Iraq, Pakistan and Bangladesh unilateral divorce is allowed, but it must be duly registered and defaulting husband is liable for punishment. It is high time that something be done in India too. It is interesting to note that under a decree of H.H. the Aga Khan, the Khojas in India have their own marriage tribunals, and neither a second marriage nor a divorce is possible without recourse to these tribunals.

A former member of National Commission for Women and founder of Muslim Women's Forum, who is a prominent scholar of the India namely Smt. Syidain Hameed has written in an article on this form of Talaq i.e Talaq-ul-Biddat and strongly recommended that" The Fact of the matter is that we Muslims selectively practice whatever suits our need. We ascribe our actions to our religious sanctions and continuously harp on our religious code. But we blatantly violate the injunctions of the Islam. We pronounce Talaq without following the commands pertaining to it. Thanks to the way we practice it. The Islam is looked upon by the world as the most anti-gender religion, for this perception, it is we Muslims who are to be blamed. It is time we applied the corrective to our own selves and stop using religion." It is common practice among Hanafi Muslims to pronounce Talaq thrice in a go impulsively, as no other school recognizes this form of Talaq. Another scholar Sakina Yusuf Khan has written in another article that "Today an ideal situation seems to be emerging instead of law Courts and reformist organizations proposing changes in the Muslim Personal Law and getting stonewalled by fundamentalists the move for change is from within the community's orthodox leadership and it must unequivocally be welcomed. "

The All India Muslim Personal Law Board, the Apex Law-making Body of Muslims on religious and personal issues, has suggested a number of reforms in marriage and divorce laws aimed at giving the community's women a better deal. The most important of the suggested changes relates to the continuous issue of triple Talaq. On this the Board's recommendation that Muslim men be "restrained" from pronouncing instant triple Talaq falls far short of expectations. Nothing short of an express ban on the obnoxious practice of Talaq-e-Bidat will make any real, difference. The Board has little reason to be diffident on this issue for it would be within the Shariat's framework. Talaq-e-Bidat which gives Muslim men absolute and unilateral power of divorce is upheld only by the Hanafi School of Islamic Jurisprudence. The other three schools - Maliki, Shafii and Hambali - do not approve of it. Besides, Talaq-e-Bidat where the very word "Bidat" means 'undesirable or forbidden innovation is not sanctioned by Quran. It was used as an emergency measure on a few occasions by Calipha Umar who later regretted allowing it.

In many Muslim countries, including Pakistan, where the majority consists of Hanafi Law followers has restricted this Un-Quranic form of Talaq. In Pakistan if a husband uses this form of talaq to divorce his wife, he has to notify an arbitration council / Shariat Court, immediately after the pronouncement of triple Talaq. Effect to such a notice is that if it would freeze the Talaq for 90 days during which time the council would try for a reconciliation and if during this period no patch up is possible then Talaq would become final. The second point where voices are being raised, concerns payment of Mehr which seldom takes place as the Quranic rules provide. Usually Mehr is deferred and even after divorce it is a long process to realize the among by the help of a Civil Court, but thanks to Muslim Women Act of 1986, which provides disposal of application of divorced wife for Mehr, reasonable and fair provision and maintenance within one month.

The other issue concerns the right of Muslim Women to divorce on her own. For this AIMPLE Board has recommended a written N ikahnama in each case where some conditions would be added to give Muslim woman a right of divorce. All these matters were discussed in detail in a general house meeting of the Board in October, 2000. In this regard Maulana Ali Naqi has suggested, within the parameters of Quranic Commands, that in the Nikahnama itself a provision could be incorporated that for purposes of Talaq, the wife would be representative (Vakil) of her husband for life. Where a need arises the wife could pronounce Talaq on behalf of her husband as his representative (Vakil). Apart from Khula it could be an additional right of wife if she chooses to do so. Fiqah does not bar such a condition in a Nikahnama or a marriage contract. Besides this Fyzee has mentioned a Nikah deed drafted by him where both the parties to marriage agree that wife has a right to divorce her husband on conditions mentioned therein. Maulana Abul Kalam Azad., in his explication of Quran (2: 228) has said that in all matters men and women have equal rights over each other. This rule is incorporated in the said Aayat's five words.

"Wala Hunna Mislullazi Alayhinna Bill-Maruul". To justify this rule, right of divorce in the form of Khula has been provided to women. It is evident that those provisions which are being demanded to be reformed, are those which had come as, 'reforms' than after death of the Prophet Mohammed. In fact, it is these reformed provisions which are creating problems and now irony of the situation is that present proposal of reforms is nothing but annulling those 'reforms' and reverting back to original Quranic Law of Shariat. Those 'reforms' had failed the test of time and proved that neither there is any anomaly in Quranic Law nor there is any need to reform them. That was the reason that nobody, how so ever spiritual by highly placed he might be, is allowed to make amends in the Shariat Law. It is pity that for hundreds of year, these wrong notions were considered as actual Shariat.

Reference:-

1 The Quran - Sura-al-Nisa
2 The Quran - Sura-al-Nisa
3 The Quran -II, 187 Translated by Mr.YusufAli
4 Arneer Ali - Mohammedan Law
5 Abdul Qadir Vs. Salirna : (1866) 8 All 149
6 M.U.S . Jung, Dissertation
7 Principles of Mohammedan Jurisprudence
8 Ameer Ali - Mohammedan Law
9 Abdul Qadir Vs. Salima: (1886) 8 All 155
10 Wilson - Anglo-Mohammedan Law
11 Mst.Ghulam Kubra Vs. Mohammad Shall: AIR (1940) Peshawar 2.3: & Mst. Zainaba Vis. Abdul Rahman: AIR (1945) Peshawar 51
12 Nawab Sadiq Ali Khan V s . Jai Kishori : (1928) 30 80m. L.R.1346
13 Allah Diwaya Vs. Kammon Mai: Pl.D 1957 (W.P.) Lah.65I
14 Dissolution of Muslim Marriage Act VIII of 1939. Section 2 (vii)
15 Nizamuddin Vs. Huseni: AIR (1960) M.P.2I2
16 Abdul Razack Vs. Aga Mohammad: (1893) 21.1A.56
17 Ameer Ali - Mohammedan Law
18 Tyabji, Faiz - Muslim Law
19 Aizunnisa Vs. Karimunnisa : (1895)23 Cal.130
20 C The Quran - IV, 23 Translated by Mr.Yusuf Ali.
21 According to Hedaya cited by Mahmood J.in Re Din Muhammad: (1882) 5 All 226, 231
22 Ameer Ali -The Fatimid Law declares a marriage during 'Idda' as void. as distinguished from being merely irregular. Fat Laws
23 Mulla - Principles of Mohammedan Law
24 in Jamait Ali Saheb Vs. Mil' Mohammed: (1916) Punjab Record
25 Khoo Hooi Leong Vs. Khoo Hean Kwel : (1926) A.C.529
26 Kadir Vs. Salima: I.L.R (1886) 8 All 149 (F.B.)
27 Abdul QadirVs. Salima : (1886) 8 All 149
28 Abdul Qadir Vs. Salima : (1886) 8 All 149

29 Anis Begam Vs. Mohd.Istefa: (1933) 55 All 743

30 Tahir Mahmood - Islamic Law in India

31 A.A.A. Fyzec - Outlines of Mohammedan Law

32 Shazada Qauram Vs. Fakher Jung : AIR 1953 (Hyd) -134

33 Fyzee - Outlines or Mohammedan Law

34 Shohrat Singh Vs. Jafri Bibi : 24 I.C. 499 P.C.

35 Maulana Mohammad Ali: In Commentary on the Holy Quran. - 96

36 Ibrahim Abdul Hamid - "Dissolution of Marriage" in Islamic Quarterly. (3) (1956) 166

37 Ameer Ali - The spirit of Islam

38 Sura 2, Al-Baqorah Aayat 228

39 Sura 2, Al-Baqurah Aayat 229

40 Sura 2, Al-Baqurah Aayat 230

41 Sura 2, Al - Baqurah Aayat 231

42 Sura 2, Al - Baqurah Aayat 232

43 Sura 2, Al - Baqurah Aayat 236

44 Sura 2, Al - Baqurah Aayat 237

45 Sura 33, Al - Baqurah Aayat 49

46 Fatwa-i-Alamgiri. Vol. I - 491

47 Wajid Ali Vs. Jaffar Hussain: AIR Oudh 34

48 Arneer Ali - Mohammedan Law II

49 The Quran IV, 127 Translated by Mr.Yusuf Ali

50 Ameer Ali - Mohammedan Law - II, 432

51 Modhi Vs. Kallendar : AIR 1927 PC 15

52 Rashid Ahumad Vs. Anisa Begum: AIR 1932 P.c. 25

53 Ful Chand Vs. Nazab Ali Choudhary: (1909) AIR 36 Cal 185; & Mohd. Shamsuddin Vis. Noor Jahan, AIR 1955 (Hyd) 144

54 Hannefa Vs. Pathummal : 1972 KLT 512

55 Fyzee - Outlines of Mohammedan Law

56 Paras Diwan - Muslim Law in Modern India

57 Fyzee - Outlines of Mohammedan Law

58 Ameer Ali - Mohammedan Law

59 Fyzee - Outlines of Mohammedan Law

60 Fazlur Rahman Vs. Aisha: 1929 I.L.R. 8 (Pat) 690

61 K.P.Sharma : Muslim Vidhi

62 Rahema Khatoon Vs. Iqtidar-ud-din : AIR 1943 (All) 184

63 Hamidoola Vs. Faizunnisa: (1812) 8 Cal.327

64 Saifuddin Vs. Lati funnisa : (1919) 46 Cal.141

65 Moonshee Buz-ul-Raheem Vs. Lateefa-un-Nissa: (1861) 8 M.I.A.379

66 Paras Diwan: Muslim in Modern India

67 Sayeeda Khanum Vs. Mohd.Sami: PLD 1952 (WP) Lah.113 (FB)

68 Fyzee - Outline of Mohammedan Law

69 Nurjahan Bibi Vs. Mohd. Kazim Ali: AIR 1977 Cal 90

70 Abdul Khadar Vs. Taib Begum: AIR 1957 Mad. 340

71 Vijay Malik - Muslim Law of Marriage. Divorce & Maintenance

72 Tufail Ahmad Vs. Jamila Khatun: 1962 All LJ. 971

73 Sham-un-Nissa Vs. Mir: AIR 1940 Cal.95

74 Ahmad Vs. Fatma: AIR 1931 80m.76

75 Kalin Vs. Mst. Imaman : AIR 1949 All 445

76 B.N.Sampath -Uniform Civil Code: Judicial Separation and Divorce

77 Tyabji - Muslim Law

78 K.C.Moyin Vs. Nafeesa : AIR 1973 Ker.176

79 Mohd. Ahmed Khan Vs. Shah Bano Begum: (1985) 2 see 556

80 Rashid Ahmad Vs. Anisa Khatun: (1931) 59 IA 21

81 The Holy Quran. Note 254 Vol. I, Translated by YusufAli

82 Koushar Ali Laskar Vs. Moslcma Bibi: 2000 (2) Cr. 1. 134

83 S.K. Kader - Muslim Law of Marriage and Succession in India

84 Shamim Ara Vs. State of U.P.: 2002 (7) SCC518

85 Jai-ud-din Ahmed Vs. Anwara Begum: 1981 (I) G.L.R. 358

86 Rukia Khatun Vs. Abdul Khalik Laskar : 1981 (I) G.L.R. 375

87 Shamim Ara Vis. State of U.P. : 2002 (7) see 518

88 Ameer Ali - Mohammedan Law

89 Abdul YusufVs. Sowramma: AIR 1971 Ker 261

90 M.R. Zafar - Unilateral Divorce in Muslim Personal Law

91 Tahir Mahmood - Family Law Reform in the Muslim World

CHAPTER-III

CHAPTER-III
Meaning, Nature and Essential Conditions of Mahr

Mahr (dower)

"And give the women their dowers as a gift spontaneous "[1]

Since a Muslim wife in marriage surrenders her person, so the husband must also surrender at least some of his property according to his means and this gives rise to the law of dower (Mahr). A minimum dower is to be prescribed but it is not necessary to stick to the minimum and in the new relationship created by the parties is recommended to act towards each other with the greatest confidence and liberty. The Mahr (dower) has been divided as per heads enumerated below:

(1) Meaning of Mahr ;

(2) Nature of Mahr ; &

(3) Essential requirements of Mahr.

(1) Meaning of Mahr

Since the historical background of Mahr has already been discussed at length in earlier chapter and thus the study shows that prior to the Islam, two kinds of marital gifts were prevalent. In a type of marriage called 'Beena' the husband visited the wife but did not bring her home. Here wife was called 'Sadiqa' or female friend and a gift given to the wife on marriage was called 'Sadaqa'. Generally Sadaqa simply means a dowry and is synonymous with Mahr. But originally the two words were quite distinct. Sadaqa is a gift to wife and Mahr to the parents of the wife, this term belongs to the marriage of dominion which is known as the 'Baal marriage', where the wife's people part with her and have to be compensated. The Holy Prophet to ameliorate the position of wife in the Islam combined it with 'Sadaqa' to that it became a settlement or a provision for wife. Mahr belongs absolutely to the wife in Islamic Law. The author of Hedaya when he says the payment of dower is enjoyment by the law merely as a token of respect for its object (the woman) wherefore the mention of it is not absolutely essential to the validity of a marriage and for the same reason a marriage is also valid.

Tyyabji[2] says Dower (Mahr) is a sum that becomes payable by the husband to the wife on marriage either by agreement between the parties or by operation of law it may be either prompt (Muajjal) or deferred (Muwajjal).

According to Mulla[3] "Dower (Mahr)" is a sum of money or other property which the wife is entitled to receive from her husband in consideration of the marriage. The word consideration is not used in the sense in which the word is used in the Indian Contract Act. It is obligation imposed upon the husband as a mark of respect to the wife. Abdur Rahim says "it is either a sum of money or other form of property to which the wife becomes entitled by marriage. It is an obligation imposed by the law on the husband as a mark of respect for the wife." The Hon'ble Justice Mahmood has said in Abdul Kadir Vs. Salima[4] Mahr in Muslim Law is a sum of money or other property promised by the husband to be paid or delivered to the wife in consideration of marriage and even where no dower is expressly fixed or mentioned at the marriage ceremony, the law confers the right of proper dower to the wife. In Saburunnisa Vs. Sabdu Shaikh[5] the Calcutta High Court has observed that Muslim marriage is like a contract of sale in which the wife is the property and dower is the price.

Ameer Ali[6] defines "Dower (Mahr) is a consideration which belongs absolutely to the wife."

Dr. M.U.S. Jung[7] in his work a digest of Anglo-Muslim Law (1932) defines 'Dower' as the property or its equivalent incumbent on the husband either by reason of being agreed in the contract of marriage or by virtue of a separate contract, as special consideration of 'Buza' the right of enjoyment itself. The Islamic concept of the Mahr (dower) is unfortunately one of the most misunderstood concept of Muslim Law. Those who lean towards the contractual element of the Muslim marriage tend to equate it with the consideration. On the other hand, those more familiar with the Indian concept dowry, confuse it with that concept. The truth is that Mahr (dower) is not a form of dowry; rather it is given as a mark of respect and love token to the wife by the husband. Thus, it is significant institution in the Islamic Law because it is given as a mark of respect and further as a love token to the wife by the husband. Thus it occupies a unique position of its own in the Islamic Law.

It is submitted that the above opinion which declares Mahr as a consideration for marriage is erroneous because in those cases where no dower is specified at the time of marriage, further the marriage is not void on that account but the law requires some dower (proper) dower should be paid to wife. Abdur Rahim's words[8] gives more clear meaning of Mahr as he says "It is not a consideration, proceeding from the husband for the contract of marriage, but it is an obligation imposed by the law on the husband as mark of respect to the wife as is evident from the fact that non specification of dower at the time of marriage doesn't affect the validity of marriage."

2. Nature of Mahr

The Mahr is a word inviting a controversy and misinterpretation as it is, has been an object of bad arguments; whereas some identifies it with a price of the: bride, consideration of marriage contract because as the Justice Mitter in Saburunnisa's[9] case confused it with dowry. The true picture is known to the people according to Quranic injunctions and through relevant Hadiths, so here an attempt has been made to know the true nature of Mahr and attitude of Indian Judiciary. These two points may be noted with respect to the nature of dower:-

(i) The wife is considered to be property and the dower to be the price and it is a consideration for conjugal intercourses; &

(ii) Dower is an essential incident and fundamental feature of marriage with the result that even if no dower is fixed the wife is entitled for proper dower from her husband.

It is submitted that it is incorrect to treat marriage as a contract in the sense which is implied in traffic or transaction of goods and services, accordingly dower cannot be treated as a consideration of that nature which is found in the case of sale and purchase of goods.

The fact is that Islamic Law bestows upon woman certain privileges because of the peculiar position she occupies and the role she has to play in an organized social set up. The general principles about the treatment of woman which emphasize the nature of the prescribed attitude in the field of family and group relationships find a prominent place in the following verses of the Holy Quran :

All mankind are one and mutual rights
must be respected, the sexes
must honour, each the other
Sacred are family relationships
That rise through marriage
And woman bearing children
Orphans need especial loving care.

Mr. Justice Mahmood, who is considered to be the pioneer of the view point that marriage amongst Muslims is purely a civil contract, is himself not sure about the question of whether dower was exactly similar to the consideration in a contract of sale and purchase of goods. He stated that it represented a property promised to be delivered to the wife in consideration of marriage. It expressly conveyed the idea that the reason of such promise was marriage alliance but it does not in any way justify its equation with the price of a commodity. Researcher is strengthened in holding this view about the correct meaning and importance of the observations of the Learned Justice Abdul Qadir by his own comments:[10]

"Dower, under Mohammedan Law, is a sum of money for or other property promised by the husband to be paid or delivered to the wife in consideration of the marriage .... the dower of the under Mohammedan Law bears a strong resemblance to the denatio propter of the Romans which has subsisted in the English Law under the name of marriage settlement. In this sense, and in no other, can dower the under Mohammedan Law be regarded as the consideration for connubial intercourse, and if the authors of the Arabic text-books of under Mohammedan Law have compared it to the price in the contract of the sale, it is simply because marriage is a civil contract under that law, and sale is the typical contract under which Mohammedan Jurists are accustomed to refer to in illustrating the incidents of other contracts by analogy. "

The above observation of the Learned Justice clarified that he used the term 'consideration' for dower by way of 'similitude' and never equated the two on the basis of their true nature. He quoted 'Hedaya' to establish that dower was not an exchange but merely an incident of the final decision between two Muslims to live as husband and wife.[11] Hedaya as quoted by Mr.Justice Mahmood explains that:

" ..... not the exchange or consideration given by the man to the woman but an effect of the contract imposed by law on the husband as a token of respectfor its subject the woman.... ..

Mr. Justice Mahmood was wrongly understood by the later decision makers who, without taking into consideration, decided different nature of a contract of sale and marriage, took the two as identical to each other. The following observation of Mr. Mahmood puts this understanding of the judgment beyond any reasonable doubt:

"The payment of dower is enjoined by the law merely as a token of respect for its object (the woman) wherefore the mention of it is not absolutely essential to the validity of a marriage, and for the same reason, a marriage is also valid, although the man was engaged in contract on special condition that there should be no dower."

The passages quoted above from Abdul Qadir's case leave no doubt the fact that though the Learned Justice declared marriage as "a purely civil contact" by accepting the passage from the Tagore Law Lectures (1873) delivered by Mr. Jadunath Sarkar, but he probably never meant that it will be treated as a contract of sale by future judicial decisions.[12] If it is held otherwise, then he will be certainly guilty of drawing perverse inferences from the materials quoted by him in support of his conclusions. Mere reference cannot determine the actual nature and place occupied by the institution of dower. As well known, various comparisons are used to clarify a particular phenomenon but they by themselves cannot be given more weight than a device of a convenience or a technique often used by the judges. The peculiar nature of certain institutions requires considerable explanations and analogous phenomena, quoted by way of examples. It will be erroneous to exactly equate an example and the institution which is explained with its help. The view that Mr. Justice Mahmood was not properly understood and followed is without doubt is a proposition justified by his own opinions expressed and pointed out earlier and probably only the obiter-dicta without the effective cause was taken as its complete import. Further the following observation may also be noted:[13]

"The marriage contract is easily dissoluble and the freedom of divorce and the rule of polygamy place a power in the hands of the man which the law given intended to restrain by rendering the rules as to payment of dower stringent upon the husband."

The Islamic Matrimonial Law as found in parent source strengthens the observation of Mr. Justice Mahmood as dower is now here treated as the price of the bride:

Except for these, all others
Are lawful, provided
Ye seek (them in marriage)
With gifts from your property
Desiring chastity, not lust
Seeing that ye derive
Benefit from the give them
Their dower (at least)
As prescribed; but if
After a dower prescribed,
ye agree Mutually (to vary it)
There is no blame on you,
And God in all knowing,
All wise

There is a long time of judicial decision where: in this reference between the two points mention and they are examined with a view to explain the characteristics of the marriage settlement known as dower. In Hamira Bibi's case[14], the Privy Council observed and finally declared that it was in fact an essential incident to the marriage.

Again, the Privy Council in Syed Sabir Hussain[15] case discussed at length the legal incidence of the institution of dower and finally concluded that it is not only a pious obligation but legal responsibility of the husband too. Another notable judgment[16] carrying the same line of thought is that of Chief Justice Sir Sulaiman wherein he implicitly acknowledged dower as a 'mark of respect' and took the cautious view that:

"The analogy of the same cannot be carried out too far. The marriage cannot be regarded as purely sale of the person of the wife in consideration for the payment of dowe."

Yet another significant and well known judicial opinion was delivered by Justice Tek Chand in Mst.Fatima Bibi Vs. Lal Din, where he categorically declared that:

"Under the Mohammedan Law dower is not exchange or consideration, as understood in the technical sense in the Contract Act, given by the man to the woman for entering into the contract but an effect of the contract imposed by the law on the husband as a token of respect for its subject, the woman. So an agreement by the third person guaranteeing payment of a post nuptial dower, is not void as being without consideration and the third person cannot escape liability under it"

He further quoted with approval the observation of Allahabad High Court in Kamar-un-Nissa Bibi Vs. Hussaini Bibi[17], in this case it was held that

" ..... It is not necessary that dower should be agreed upon before marriage, it may be fixed afterwards ...."

The High Court conclusively held that

"Consideration not to be taken or has been used in the Indian Contract Act."

And in support of this observation the Learned Judge referred to Sir Abdur Rahim[18] that

" .....A marriage is valid though dower is not settled at the time and it is wrong to say that dower is consideration proceeding from the husband for the contract of marriage. In reality it is an obligation imposed by Mohammedan Law as a mark of respect for the wife..........."

So the comparison between 'dower' and 'consideration' is mere analogical and the one is not an identical precedent for the other. It will be wrong to scratch the analogy of sale too far. Marriage is neither a contract of sale in the strict sense, nor the consideration of marriage that is known as dower. It is really surprising as to how the courts still treat marriage as a transaction of a sale inspite of weighty judicial precedents to the contrary the realities of human mind appear to have worked against the true nature of institution of marriage and dower and judicial sphere of decision making. As is evident from the observation of Mr. Justice Mitter in Subrannisa Vs. Sabdu Sheikh[19] and the opinion of Hon'ble Mr. Mookerjee and Amiya Kumar J.J. in B.M. Mondal Vs. D.R. Bibi.[20] It is virtually the outcome of the decision of Abdul Qadir's case. It was observed by Sir Suleman in Wajid Ali Khan's case that similarly of dower to sale price cannot be pushed too far, no can the principles governing the sales of goods be applied in all their details; for example the contract of sales of goods can be cancelled if a portion of the price has not been paid even if the goods have not been delivered they may in such an event be returned. But if consummation of marriage has taken place and a part of the dower remains unpaid, it would be absurd to think that marriage could be cancelled by the wife at her will.

Now, one question arise after the above discussion - Whether the dower is a consideration for the first consummation of marriage only or whether it is a consideration for wife during the married life?

The question could not be answered by applying the analogy of sale to dower money and marriage. The Islam insists that dower should be paid to the wife herself. It seeks to make dower in to a real settlement in favour of the wife, a provision for the rainy day and socially, a check on the capricious exercise by the husband of his almost unlimited power of divorce. In the words of A.A.A. Fyzee[21] "A husband thinks thrice before divorcing a wife when he knows that upon divorce the whole of the dower would be payable immediately." There is a classic example given by some one which must be mentioned here. A person purchases a horse. To whom he must pay the price? Not to the horse itself: certainly, but to owner. Thus, if dower is regarded as sale price, it must be paid to the father or the guardian of the wife since it is paid to the wife herself: it cannot be the price. It is a token of respect.

The another aspect regarding the nature of Mahr is discussed in the chapter 'Mahr as an unsecured debt' itself.

3. Essential requirements of Mahr:-

The essential requirements of the Mahr (dower) can be examined under following points:-

(A). Contractual capacity for Mahr

(B). Subject of Mahr

(A) Contractual capacity for Mahr:-

(a) Right to make a contract of Mahr - Any person who has attained majority and is of sound mind may enter into a contract of Mahr either directly or through an authorised agent.

(b) Agency for a contract of Dower - A contract of Mahr may be made on behalf of a minor husband or wife by a guardian or his agent.

(c) Mahr in writing is not necessary - A contract of Mahr may be made either orally or in writing.

(a) Right to make a contract of Mahr

A major and sound person can enter into a contract of Mahr. In Muslim Law when a person attains puberty, he becomes major to act in the matters of Marriage, Dower, and Divorce. According to Hedaya stated that the earliest age of puberty in respect to a boy is 12 and in respect to a girl is 9. In Sadiq Ali Vs. Jaikishor [22] the Privy Council observed that as per the Mohammedan Law, the age of puberty is 9 years. According to Abu Yusuf that "the age of puberty presumed to be attained at the age of 15 both for males and females" A report shows that Abu Handa and Shafei also agree with it. There are numbers of cases in support of this view Nawab Bibi Vs. Allah Ditta[23]. Mst.Ghulam Kubra Vs. Mohd. Shafi,[24] & Atiqa Begum Vs. Mohd. Ibrahim [25]

Shia Law

In this matter Shia Law says that in concern with male members puberty is presumed to be attained at the age of 15 in concern with females puberty is established at the age of 9. It begins with menstruation and presumption is that, it commence between the age of 9 and 10. Ameer Ali[26] says that it is presumed at 15 both in cases of Hanafi and Shia.

In Mohammedan Law majority for all purposes held to be attained at the age of puberty. In certain matters namely marriage dower, divorce, the provisions of Mohammedan Law is not affected by the Indian Majority Act as they have been expressly accepted by Section 2 of the Act. In all question relating to these matters the age of majority will be governed by Mohammedan Law. As per Section 2 and 3 of the Indian Majority Act are as follows :-

Section 2 of the Act that nothing herein contained shall effect: -

(i) to the capacity of any person to act in the following matters, namely, Marriage, Dower, Divorce and Adoption; or

(ii) the religion or religious rights and usages of any class of her Majesty's subjects in India; or

(iii) the capacity of any person who before this Act comes into force, has attained majority under the law applicable to him.

Section 3 of the Act that every minor of, whose person or property or both, a guardian other than a guardian for a suit within the meaning of Chapter XXXI of the Code of Civil Procedure has been or shall be appointed or declared by any Court of Justice before the minor has attained the age of 18 years and every minor of whose property the superintendence has been or shall be assumed by any 'Court of Wards' before the minor has attained that age shall notwithstanding anything contained in the Indian Succession Act (X of 1865) or any other enactment, be deemed to have attained his majority when he shall have completed the age of 21 years and not before.

Now, it is submitted that 'acting in the matter of marriage' means entering into a contract of marriage. If a Muslim minor who is a major by his Personal Law but a minor under the Indian Majority Act enters into a marriage as he is capable of doing, he must enter into a contract for payment of dower, even if, he does not do so, the law will presume such contract. In respect of a Muslim girl she attains majority under the Muslim Law on attaining puberty or on attaining the age of 15 years, whichever is earlier. It has been held that in spite of the provisions of Order XXXII of the Civil Procedure Code, a Muslim woman who is major according to her Personal Law but minor according to the Majority Act may sue without next friend in the matter of Divorce, Dower & etc. On this point there is a decision in Naksetan Bibi Vs. Habibar Rahaman[27] a decision by Justice Akram, who held that a Muslim girl who has attained puberty is herself competent to sue for dissolution of marriage without a next friend as required by Order-XXXII; Rule 1 of the Code of Civil Procedure although she may be below 18 years of age. His Lordship followed a decision of the Bombay High Court of Ahmed Sulaiman Vohra Vs. Bai Fatima a decision by Division Bench, where it was held that the Mohammedan Law entitled a woman of 16 and over to sue for a divorce. Under Section 2 (a) of Majority Act, nothing in that Act shall affect the capacity of any person to act in Marriage, Dower, Divorce and Adoption. The wife suing for a divorce, therefore, she was entitled to sue without a guardian. The same principles were followed by Justice Das Gupta, In Achia Khatoon Vs. Abdul Hai.[28] It has been held in Bombay and Calcutta that a woman of 16 and over to sue for a divorce is entitled to sue without guardian, but the contrary view has been expressed in Oudh that Order-XXXII; Rule 1 Civil Procedure Code applies and a suit for dower must be instituted through a next friend unless majority is attained under the Majority Act. It is submitted that the former view is not sound. It has also been held in Rangoon that majority is to be determined by the Majority Act in the matter of pre-nuptial agreement to contract a marriage in the future. In all other matters Gifts, Wakfs, Wills etc. majority will be determined according to Section 3 of the Majority Act [sub section (2) and (3) of this section] and not Muslim Law. Thus for purposes of appointment as a guardian for the person or property of minor, majority will be attained only after attainment of 18 years or 21 years of age, as the case may be, but for the purposes of guardianship for marriage, majority will be attained on puberty.

(b) Agency for a contract of Mahr (dower)

According to Ameer Ali[29] an agency for a contract of dower stands almost on the same footings as agency for other contracts and Mr.B.R.Verma in his commentaries on Mohammedan Law says Section 100 (1) that a guardian for marriage or his agent may contract a marriage for minor or lunatic and in Section 100 (2) a guardian may also enter into contract of dower which shall be binding on the portion provided that where the contact has been made by any guardian other than the father or grand father for inadequate dower on behalf of the wife or extravagant dower on behalf of the husband, the contract will not be binding and proper dower shall be recoverable. According to Abu Hanifa a contract would be binding even though the father of a girl has agreed to a very inadequate dower. According to disciples, the dower would be illegal only if the excess or deficiency as the case may be is very disproportionate but not otherwise. The contract by any other guardian would not be valid if it is in adequate or excessive.

Shia Law - The father and grand father are the only guardian. A contract of dower would accord to better opinion, be valid even though it is for much smaller than proper dower.

Shafei Law - The guardian of the husband can not contract a higher dower than proper dower nor can the father or grand father of the wife who can contract a marriage without her consent agree to a dower smaller than the proper dower. The wife would be entitled to proper dower in such cases.

If the agent commits fraud in fixing the dower

(i) the whole dower would be payable if before consummation either or both parties knew the fraud or the husband knew it but the wife not knew till after consummation.

(ii) only the authorised amount would be payable if the wife came to know of it before consummation and husband after that.

(c) Mahr in writing is not necessary

It is not necessary that a contract of dower should be in writing. In cases of contracts for large dower, strong evidence would be necessary.

B. Subject of' Mahr (dower)

Money or any specified thing or right which has come value may be the subject of Mahr (dower) provided that such things or right is in existence and is not such as prohibited by the religion and is not opposed to the policy of the Mohammedan Law. It is not necessary that dower should be only tangible property. What ever comes with the term 'Mal' can be the subject matter of dower. Every thing corpored except Carrion and Blood is 'Mal'. Any thing which has some value and that is not prohibited under Mohammedan Law is 'Mal' and can be a subject matter of Mahr for example-Insurance Policies, chooses-in-action, profits arising from land or business, debts due to the husband from the wife herself or from others, the sale-proceeds of some things of which the husband is a proprietor can constitute valid dower. According to Bailie, that which is not 'Mal' as that the husband will not take her out of her native place or will perform 'Haj' with her cannot be the subject of dower. Things which are prohibited by religion as hogs or wine are not valid subjects of Mahr. Further the things which are not in existence, the future produce of some trees or flocks in the womb, can not be the subject of dower. In Shia Law the usufruct of property not in existence, contingent benefits, may be valid subject of dower.

Payment to the father - In a condition if a husband promised that he would give some thing to the father of the bride would not be valid as a subject of dower. In such cases, the wife would be entitled to proper dower. In Shia Law, if the Mahr is specified for the woman and also some thing for the father, the husband is bound only for the first and the stipulation in favour of the father is of no avail. According to Shia and Shafai the rendering of personal service including teaching of Quran is a valid forum of dower, if the time is specified and there is no uncertainty. According to Hedaya the husband may here some one to perform the service.

It is observed that Islamic matrimonial history provides evidence that the Holy Prophet Mohammed was never ready to hand over a woman to a man without the payment of dower. An incident is reported with slight difference between the Shia and Sunni authorities that a woman come to the Prophet Mohammed and stood before him saying "O Messenger of Allah", said she "accept me your wife". The Prophet Mohammed in respect of the request of the woman, kept silence and said nothing. The woman set down in her place. One of his companions stood up and said, "O messenger of Allah, if you are not ready I am prepared to accept her as my wife." The Holy Prophet

Mohammed asked "what do you submit as a dower "I have not got any thing was the reply." This can not be, go to your house, perhaps you will find some thing there to give as a dower to his woman. "The Prophet Mohammed said the man went to his house" came back and said, "I could not find any thing in my house." The Prophet Mohammed said "Go again and look well." If you can find a metal ring, even that would suffice." said the Prophet Mohammed. He went twice and came back and said, "I cannot find even a metal ring in my house." I am ready to present her with clothes that I am wearing as dower. Another companion who knew the man said, "o messenger of Allah, by Allah, this man has no other clothes except those he is wearing. So help of the clothes may be assigned as the dower of the woman. The Prophet Mohammed said, "if half of these clothes are to be dower of the woman, who would wear which half? If one of wears them, the other will remain undressed. No, it is cannot be like this." The man who had made the request sat down. The woman also waited in her place. The gathering took up some other topic and the discussion lasted for a long time. The man who had requested the hand of the woman started to go away, but the Prophet Mohammed called him. "Come over here" He came, "Speak, tell me, can you recite some of the Sura? "Can you recite memory?" Yes, I can "Very good" Now, it is all right. So, I marry this woman to you, and her dower will be that you teach her the Quran. The man took the hand of the woman and went away.

The fittings subject-matter of dower is not only confused to a sum of money or property it includes personal services and other thing. According to a tradition Aamir-Bin-Rabia said "that a woman of the tribe of Bani-Fajarah married on a settlement of a pair of shoes, and the Prophet Mohammed said to her "Are you pleased to give yourself and your property for those two shoes." She said 'Yes' Then the Prophet Mohammed approved of the marriage. The following were recognized as the subject of dower:-

(i) A handful of dates[30] (Abu Daud)

(ii) A pair of shoes[31] (Tirmizi)

(iii) If the husband is a slave, his services to his wife:[32] (Mohit Sarkhsee)

(iv) The services of the husband slave to the wife[33] (Fatwa -i Alamgiri)

(v) Husband services rendered to the guardian of a minor wife[34] (Darrul Muktar)

(vi) Teaching Quran to the wife (Tradition)

In fact, the main contention of the Muslim Justice is that any thing which comes within the definition of 'Mal' can be the subject matter of dower. If the subject matter of dower be "an animal" or "cloth" then the wife is entitled to Mahr-ul-Misl (proper dower) because such dower is invalid for uncertainty. Similarly, "a house' or 'the land" without specify, court will. Here mention of Nikah-us-Shighar is necessary. It is a practice in have to fix proper dower in such cases. Which a person contracts his daughter or his sister in marriage to another on the condition of other bestowing as sister or daughter in marriage upon him, so that each contract shall stand as return for the others, this will not be sufficient in place of dower. In such cases both the marriage would be valid and each wife would be entitled to proper dower. In Shia Law and Shafai Law, the contract of marriage would be void. But such marriages become valid after consummation and proper dower would be due in each case.

Reference:-

1 The Quran-IV: 24. Translated by Mr. Yusuf Ali

2 Tyyabji. Faiz - Muslim Law

3 Mulla - Principles of Mohammedan Law

4 Abdul Kadir Vs. Salima: (IR86) 8 A1149

5 Saburunnisa Vs. Sabdu Shaikh: AIR 1934 (Cal) 693

6 Ameer Ali - Mohammedan Law

7 Dr. M.U.S.Jung - A Digest of Anglo Muslim Law (1932)

8 Abdur Rahim - Mohammedan Jurisprudence

9 Saburunnisa Vs. Sabdu Sheikh: AIR 1934 (Cal) 693

10 Abdul Qadir Vs. Salima: (1886) 8 All 149

11 Ibid

12 Nizamuddin Vs. Husimi : AIR 1960 MP 212; & Haji Mokshed Mandai Vs Del Rushon Bibi : AIR 1971 (62) Cal. 162

13 Fyzee AAA : Cases in the Mohammedan Law of India and Pakistan, page-III (1965)

14 Hamira Bibi Vs. Zubaida : 43 I.A .294

15 Syed Sabir Hussain Vs. Farzand Hussain : AIR 1933 PC 80

16 Anis Begum Vs. Mohammad Istafa : (1933) 55 All 755

17 Kamar-un-Nissa Bibi Vs, Hussaini Bibi : (1881) 3;All 266 (PC)

18 Abdur Rahim - Mohammedan Jurisprudence

19 Subrannisa Vs. Sabdu Sheikh : AIR 1934 Cal. 693

20 B.M. Mondal Vs. D,R, Bibi : AIR 1971 Cal. 162

21 Fyzee, A.A.A. - Outlines of Mohammedan Law

22 Sadiq Ali Vs. laikishor : AIR 1928 (PC) 152

23 Nawab Bibi Vs. Allah Ditta: AIR 1924 Lah. 188

24 Mst.Ghulam Kubra Vs. Mohd. Shaf : AIR 1940 Pcshwer 2

25 Atiqa Begum V s. Mohd. Ibrahim: AIR 1916 PC 250 & 36 IC

26 Ameer Ali - Moharnrnedan Law

27 Naksetan Bibi Vs. Habibar Rahaman : 50 C.W.N. 689

28 Achia Khatoon Vs. Abdul Hai : AIR 1931 Bom 76

29 Ameer Ali - Mohammedan Law

30 Abu Daud

31 Tirmizi

32 Mohit Sarkhswee

33 Fatwa-i-Alamairi

34 Durrul Muktal

CHAPTER-IV

CHAPTER-IV
Classification of the Mahr

(1) Specified Mahr (AI - Mahr - al - Musamma)

(2) Unspecified Mahr (Mahr - al - Mithal / Proper Mahr)

(1) Specified Mahr (AI - Mahr - al - Musamma)

And lawful for you are all woman besides those.
provided that you seek keen with your property,
taking them in marriage,
not committing fornication then as to,
those idioms you profit (by marriage),
Give them their dower as appointed.[1]

It would appear from this that the Holy Quran renders the payment of dower necessary at the time of marriage. The payment of dower was necessary even though it might be a very small sum. In some exceptional cases, marriage is a legal even though, the amount of dower has not been specified at the time of 'Nikah ' but it is obligatory and must be paid afterwards. The Holy Quran says:

There is no blame on you,
if you divorce women,
you have not touched them
or appointed for them a dower.

This study shows that marriage is valid without specifying dower. Tradition also speaks of the validity of a marriage, even though no mention of dower is made at the time of consummation of marriage or afterwards. The amount of dower in this case would depend upon the circumstances of the husband and the position of the wife. The Holy Quran makes this clear by requiring the provisions for wife that it depends upon the circumstances of the husband. The Holy Quran says:

"The wealthy according to his means
and the straitened according to his means "

The payment of dower on the part of the husband is an admission of the independence of the wife as she becomes the owner of property immediately on the marriage, though before that, she may not have owed any thing. The setting of a dower on the woman at the time of marriage is obligatory.

Now these days, the practices is generally that the dower has an aspect of a guarantee and undertaking that, the man make an agreement for a certain amount in the term of dower, in favour of his wife, but the woman does not generally demand it, except on the occasion of difference or dispute that might arise between them. This kind of dower can transfer itself into a security. So it can infer from the Quranic verses and relevant Hadiths that under Mohammedan Law, dower is an incident of marriage which is backbone of the society and later jurists divided dower into two parts. One is called Mahr-i-Muajjal that is immediately eligible or prompt and other Mahr-i-Muawjjal that is deferred depends upon on the contracts of parties and the absence of any contract on the custom of the country. Ameer Ali[2] said that in any condition there can be no marriage without Mahr. Dower may be either specified or not specified. In latter case it is called Mahr-al-Mithal, proper dower or to be strictly literal, the dower of the like. If the dower has been specified then the question may be whether, it is prompt (Muajjal) or deferred (Muwajjal)

Now, it is submitted that there are two kinds of dower in Mohammedan Law:

(1) Specified Mahr (AI - Mahr - al - Musamma)

(2) Unspecified Mahr (Proper Mahr or Customary Mahr, Mahr - al - Mithal)

The Specified Mahr may again divided into

(a) Prompt Dower - Mahr - i - Muajjal

(b) Deferred Dower - Mahr - i - Muwajjal

(1) Specified Mahr (Al - Mahr - al - Musamma)

Usually the Mahr is fixed at the time of Nikah and the Qazi performing the ceremony enters the amount in register or there may be regular contract called Kabinnama with other numerous conditions. The sum may be fixed either at the time of marriage or later on and a father's contract on behalf of a minor son is binding on the minor. The wife is entitled to recover such dower which is called specified dower. This specified dower may be fixed either before or at the time of the marriage or after the marriage. Dower can be had as consideration for past as also future cohabitation.[3] The guardian may also make such a contract on behalf of a minor son.[4] If a marriage is made on the condition that dower would be fixed later on then unless the parties agree as to the amount fixed, the specified dower would not be :

(i) less than the proper dower, if it is to be fixed by the husband; &

(ii) more than the proper dower if it is to be fixed by the wife.

If the dower is left to be specified by any other person the wife would be entitled only to her proper dower unless the parties agree.

Shia Law - In such cases the husband may fix any amount, he pleases but the wife is not entitled to fix more than the Mahr-as-Sunnat that means not more than (500 Dirhams).

The Mahr-al-Musamma may also be increased at any time after it is fixed. An addition to dower may be made even after a relinquishment of dower. An addition made during the period of Iddat in the case of irrevocable divorce would be valid. But any addition after separation would be void. A post nuptial agreement of dower requires the concurrence of both the parties. It must be an offer by the husband and acceptance by the wife or by her guardian. On behalf of her an addition to dower is not a gift requiring delivery of possession to render it complete.

Shafei Law - According to Shafei Law any additions to dower are treated as gifts. The conditions for a valid gift including delivery of possession must be complied with. An addition without seisin is therefore, not valid. The amount of dower is ordinarily fixed by oral contract, and this is valid. There is also no limit either to the maximum or minimum of the amount of dower, although the early Hanafi lawyers had fixed ten Dirhams as the minimum for it and the Malik has considered even a smaller sum as permissible. These minimum have now become obsolete and the amount of dower depends entirely upon other considerations, such as the circumstances of the husband and the wife, the necessity of a device to prevent on the part of the husband the arbitrary exercise of the power of divorce vested in him, the position of the paternal family of the woman, her intellectual attainments or personal attractions and qualifications, wealth of her husband, conditions of society surrounding her and the desire of self-glorification and vanity on the part of the parties. All these considerations enter into the determination and settlement of the amount of dower.[5] Mr. Ameer Ali[6] in his Mohammedan Law, has observed as follows, "In India, for example among the upper middle class, the amount of dower ranges from Rs. 4,000- to Rs. 40,000. In Bihar, the latter is, generally speaking the customary dower, in Lower Bengal, there is no custom. Among the lower classes" the Mahr varies from Rs.50/- to Rs.400/-. In princely families, the dower consists of several Lakhs Rupees. Indeed the excess in dower amount had become so oppressive and unjust to the children of a Muslim by a predeceased wife that in 1876 an Act called Oudh Laws Act was made, whereby Section 5 thereof the civil court was given power to fix a reasonable amount of dower where the amount of dower stipulated in any contract of marriage by a Muslim was excessive with reference to the means of the husband. In such a contingency the entire sum provided in the contract was not to be awarded in any suit by decree in favour of the plaintiff, or by allowing it by the way of set-off, lien or otherwise to the defendant. The amount of dower to be allowed by the court was to be reasonable with reference to the means of the husband and the status of the wife. In the case of Nujumooden Ahmed Vs.Beebee Hoosienee,[7] there are observations to the effect that Mohammedan dower being the consideration paid by the bridegroom for the marriage, should be taken and to be regulated by the position and conduct of the bride especially because the Mohammedans often contract most unequal marriages. It is also recognised that when there is no written contract and a dispute arises, at any time regarding the amount of dower, the Mahr-ul-Misl (dower of the equals) ought to be taken as the standard by which the respective allegations of the parties are to be rested. In the case of Ekram Hussain Vs. Ali Hussain,[8] it was held by the Patna High Court that the customary dower in Bihar among Mohammedans of good class is Rs. 40,000/-. It appears further that in that case also one of the parties contended that the dower fixed was only Rs.500, but the above noted statement of Mr. Ameer Ali was referred to and also the fact that the dower of the first wife of the defendant in that suit, had been fixed at Rs.40,000 and that was considered a very important circumstance in favour of the plaintiff, the second wife of the defendant, to prove her claim that her dower had also been settled at Rs.40,000. In the case of Kulsambi Vs. Bilankhan[9], it was observed that it was not uncommon for the dower of a Muslim wife to be fixed at a figure, which was out of all proportion to the husband's means. In that case the wife claimed that her dower had been fixed at Rs.50,000, 100 Ashrafis and 50 Dinars. This was accepted on the basis of the evidence of three witnesses who were examined in proof of this fact. There was no documentary evidence. In the case of Zakeri Begum Vs. Sakina Begum[10], the Privy Council had also recognized the fact that dower was often high among Mohammedans, to prevent the husband divorcing his wife, in which case he would have to pay the amount stipulated.

Hanafi Law - The Hanafi recognizes the minimum limit of 10 Dirhams. If the dower is less than 10 Dirhams, the dower must be made up to that amount.

Value of 10 Dirhams - The question of the value of 10 Dirhams is a matter of uncertainty. In fact Dirhams of several descriptions seems to have been current at different places. The value has not been finally decided. Mr. Ameer Ali says that its value is about 5 Shillings. Mr. Macnaghten says, that the value of 10 Dirham, according to one account, is 6s 8d. The value of 10 Dirham is between Rs.3 and Rs. 4 according to an Allahabad[11] case of Asma Bibi Vs. Abdul Samad. In Sughra Vs. Masuma[12] the value of 10 Dirham was fixed at Rs.107 and Mst. Jaddo Begum Vs. Nawab Sharf Jehan Begum[13] the value of 500 Dirham was fixed at Rs.110. The value is still uncertain. But, it is a silver coin containing 2.97 Grams of silver and the best course would seem to be to calculate the value according to the price of silver of that quantity.

Shia and Shafei Law - In these schools of Muslim Law there is no fixed legal minimum for dower. Any thing which is not totally destitute of value like a grain of wheat can be fixed as dower.

No upper limit for fixing dower while the law fixes a minimum limit for dower, there is no maximum limit prescribed under this law too. According to better opinion, there are no bounds to the quantity or value of the dower. Moderation is commendable and the fixing of dower according Mahr-as-Sunnat i.e. 500 Dirhams. As it is mentioned above that there no any upper limit for fixing amount of Mahr so usually huge dowers are often fixed in case of Muslim marriages in India and such dower is a legal debt even if it is beyond the means of the husband, and even though nothing may be left to his heirs after payment of the amount. The Court is bound to allow the amount settled between the parties, even if it is excess of the fortune which the husband possessed at the time of the marriage or was expected to acquire. The Court has no power to decrease the contracted amount. The absence of such a power has been judicially deplored. A court may reduce the dower in the Mahr in there two circumstances.

Mahr-as-Sunnat

(i) when the Mahr is a fictitious one; and

(ii) when the court is empowered to do so by any special law.

Mahr-as-Sunnat or Mahr Taljii

A case of excessive Mahr and a case of fictitious dower. Mahr-as -Sunnat (Mahr Taljii) both are different. The meaning of Sunnat is sound or fame and infinitive of the verb 'be heard.' In many cases the parties settle privately a small amount of dower merely for show and family pride a large sum is mentioned although the parties do not intend to payor exact such large amount. If the parties have really contracted for a high amount of dower, the court must award it but if the contract of dower has been made for a smaller sum and a bigger sum is given out simply for the purposes of show, and then the court will be entitled to reduce the amount to that actually settled as may be possible payable. The court can hold that such contract is sham, and not the real one. Here it is submitted that the onus of proving the fictitious nature of the dower is on the party making the allegation as to its fictitious nature.

If the terms of a fictitious dower have been reduced for writing in the form of a deed, the question will arise whether the party setting up the fictitious nature of the dower is entitled to lead evidence as to its real nature and to prove that dower actually settled was not what was shown in the written deed. Will it be barred by the provisions of Sections 91 and 92 of the Indian Evidence Act.? It is submitted that it will not be barred. When the court is empowered to do so by any special law - The courts in Oudh and Ajmer-Merwara are invested with discretionary power to reduce excessive dowers and in Oudh where the Court is of opinion that the dower is excessive with reference to the means of the husband, it has the power to reduce it Under Section 5 of the Oudh Laws Act XVIII of 1876 which is as follows "Where the amount of dower stipulated in any contract of marriage by a Mohammedan is excessive with reference to the means of the husband, the entire sum provided in the contract shall not be awarded in any suit by decree in favour of the plaintiff or by allowing it by way of a set-off line or otherwise to the defendant, but the amount of dower to be allowed by the court shall be reasonable with reference to the means of the husband and the status of the wife." Further it is submitted that the courts have discretion to reduce excessive dowers to reasonable amounts. However, no reduction can be made where a decree has been passed and the matter has passed out of the stage of contract, and dower has become of the debt of record. It is necessary to mention that it is only the courts administering law in Oudh which can put into force the provisions of the Oudh Act. The Act will not apply to a case in which a Muslim residing outside Oudh marries in Oudh a woman residing in Oudh. The means of the husband which have to be considered are those which he has at the time of enforcement of the dower claim and not at the time of marriage.

Where a claim is made on a written contract and Kabinama is not proved, the court not be justified in decreeing the claim upon an oral contract not alleged in the plaint nor admitted by the defendant. Where a suit is based on a Kabiama which is not produced, its non-production must be satisfactorily accounted for or the deed must be proved by secondary evidence of a reliable nature. Generally the entries made in a register of marriages kept in discharge of duties are relevant evidence, Under Section 32 (2) of the Evidence Act as to the dower fixed. In India marriages often take place in the presence of many male persons and the wife is often of a tender age and does not have direct knowledge of the proceedings for settlement of dower. The dower is naturally arranged by her relatives. In such cases the mere fact that the plaintiff has not come into the witness box ought not to be construed against her when other relatives come into the witness box. If however there is no satisfactory explanation, the omission to appear in the witness box will tell very strongly against her whole case. Where there is a dispute as to the amount of dower, the question may have to be decided as to what amount had been specified, claim to dower is established by evidence in the same manner as other claims. A decision should be made in favour of the party which adduces evidence of the right, if both parties and neither of them adduce evidence, proper dower must be paid. In such cases proper dower may be taken as the standard for testing the respective allegations of the parties. The version which is nearer the proper dower may be accepted as the most probable. It has been held by the Privy Council in Mst.Bibi Bachun Vs. Sheikh Hamid[14] that if there is no evidence as to the agreed amount of dower, an enquiry as to the usual amount of the dower in the family (proper dower) and that is proper dower would be necessary. But in some cases it has been held that where no definite amount of dower is proved to have been fixed, what is payable is Sharai Mhar. By Sharai dower is meant the dower of 500 Dirhams given by the Holy Prophet Mohammed to all his wives except one. This is known as Mahr-as-Sunnat. It has also been held in some cases that if it is admitted that the dower was specified, but there is no satisfactory evidence of it, the burden of proof being on the wife, only the amount admitted by the husband to have been settled may be allowed. It is submitted that the principle of Mohammedan Law as to proper dower being the standard of probability.

Proper Mahr

Ye are one from mother
wed them with the leaves of their owners
and give them their dowers

according to what is reasonable

The Holy Prophet Mohammed also declared that the best among you are those who are kindest of their wives and Hazrat Ali says:

"There can be no marriage without dower. "

It is submitted that "Mahr plays an important role in the marital relationship of the husband and wife." It is a cardinal right of Muslim wife guaranteed by the Holy Quran and Prophet Mohammed, as It is submitted in previous chapter of this thesis that the Mahr regarded as a necessary incident of marriage. It is to say that if at the time of Nikha the Mahr is not fixed, the husband is bound to pay proper Mahr to his wife. In Syed Sabir Hussain's case[15] - It was held that the obligation to pay the Mahr is a legal responsibility on the part of the husband and is not dependent upon any contract between the parties; in other words, if marriage then Mahr, where there is a marriage there must be exists Mahr too.

The amount of Mahr is actually settled at the time of the marriage but in some cases Mahr is not so specified. The wife does not lose her right to get it and she will get what is called "Proper Dower or Mahr-i-Misl." One aspect of dower beneficial to the Muslim woman is that even where the parties to the marriage have not stipulated any dower, the husband remains under an obligation to pay it. Only under the Ithna Ashari Law an adult wife can waive the requirement of dower under other schools of Muslim Law, even where the wife stipulates that she will not demand any dower, she remains entitled to it and the rule of estoppel will not apply to her.

This implied dower is usually called proper dower / customary dower or Mahr-i-Misl / Mahr-ul-Misl.

One aspect of Mahr beneficial to the Muslim woman is that even where the parties to the marriage have not stipulated any dower, the husband remains under an obligation to pay it. It is important to mention here that only under the Ithna Ashari Law an adult wife can waive the requirement of dower. Under another school of Muslim Law, even where the wife stipulates that she will where the wife stipulates that she will not demand any dower she remains entitled to it and the rule of estoppel will not apply to her. This implied dower is usually called proper dower or customary dower of Mahr-i-Misl or Mahr-ul-Misl. In such case where no agreement exists, what may be those, principles upon which the amount of Mahr is to be determined usually the customary or proper dower of a woman is to be fixed with reference to the social position of her father's family and her own personal qualifications. The social position of the husband and his means are of little account. The Hedaya lays down the important rule that age, beauty; fortune, understanding and virtue must be taken into consideration. It can be said that an Islamic marriage usually safeguards the rights of a wife and attempt to ensure her an economic status consonant with her own social standing. In Abdul Rahman Vs. Mst.Inayator[16] it was held that no fixed rule can be laid down as to the determination of the amount of proper dower. It will have to be determined with due regard to a numbers of facts. It must be adjudged on definite principles. The circumstances which have to be taken into consideration in determining the amount of proper dower are:

The position of her father's family

No regard is to be paid to the dower of the mother of the wife unless she happens to be of her father's family that is (a paternal cousin) ifher mother is of her father.

Her own personal qualification

To determine the amount of proper dower attention must be paid to her equality with women from whose dowers the rule is to be taken, in point of age, beauty, fortune, understanding and virtue, because Mahr varies according to any difference in these circumstances.

The dower settled for her female paternal relations. It means the dower of (her consanguine sister, paternal aunts, cousins must be taken in to consideration to decide a proper dower for her) If there is no full or consanguine sister or paternal aunt, the dowers of the uterine sister's daughter, or uncle's daughters may be considered.

The position of the husband - The position of the husband can not be altogether excluded from consideration in determining the amount of proper dower. The financial status, and earning capacity also play an important role for proper dower. In a case name Marina Jalos Vs. Nuruddin Jatoi,[17] a Muslim married a Christian woman in England. The court observed that the marriage was governed by Muslim Law, and therefore, the husband could divorce his wife by Talaq. The court also held that the wife in turn could also claim dower, although no dower was initially fixed the time of marriage. In such case proper dower could be claimed and dower which would payable to a woman of similar status and circumstances. In other schools of Mohammedan Law such as in Ithna Ashari Law the proper dower can never exceed 500 Dirhans, the dower fixed for the Prophet Mohammed's daughter Fatima. Among Shites there are three kinds of Mahr (dower) :

(i) Mahr-e-Sunnat, the dower supported by traditions 500 Dirham.

(ii) Mahr-e-Mithal, the dower of the like or the dower of an equal, which is the technical name for proper or unspecified dower and

(iii) Mahr-e-Musamma, the specified dower.

Prompt Dower (Muajjal) & Deferred Dower (Muwajjal)

When Mahr is fixed, it is usually split into two equal parts and to stipulate that one shall be paid at once or on demand and the other on the death of the husband or on divorce or on the happening of some specified event. The technical terms for prompt dower is (Mahr-i-Muajjal) it is derived from a root meaning 'to hasten, to proceed. The term Muajjal therefore, means 'that which has been hastened or given priority in point of time.

The term Muajjal, however, means 'delayed, deferred, and comes from a root which means to delay or postpone. If it is written in the original Arabic there would be no cause for confusion, but in the English forms of spelling the words often creates confusion for those who are not so familiar with Arabic tongue. The prompt dower is payable immediately after the marriage if demanded by the wife, whereas deferred dower is payable on the dissolution of the marriage or on the happening of a specific event. The whole deferred dower becomes payable on the pronouncement of Talaq even though revocable and it does not become deferred by retention. Even revocable Talaq would hasten the payment of deferred dower, that is make it prompt and though the wife should be actually recalled by her husband. It would not again become deferred although there is also another opinion that it does not become payable till the expiry of Iddat. Which by itself indicates that unless the whole dower was prompt it could not have been stated in the deed to be due as deferred dower is not due until dissolution of marriage either by death or by divorce; and where the wife had been demanding the entire dower debt her demand could not have been made until the whole dower was prompt.

The wife is entitled to realize it any time. A previous demand and refusal is not necessary for maintaining a suit even if the amount of prompt dower is unascertained. The payment of even prompt dower is often postponed till the dissolution of the marriage but the wife is under no obligation to demand it at any time during covertures. She is entitled to recover her prompt dower at any time before or after consummation of marriage or living with the husband is not a necessary condition before it can be claimed. It is the absolute right of the wife to recover her prompt dower and while it may be open for the husband to enforce his rights in a suit for restitution of conjugal rights, prompt dower can not be made conditional on the wife's residing with the husband.

(a) Prompt Dower - Mahr - i - Muajjal

The prompt dower becomes due as soon as the marriage contract is made and it is payable when demanded by the wife. The deed of gift was executed in lieu of the dower debt of the wife. In practice, however, it is seldom paid promptly at the time of marriage or even when demanded, and equally tardily demanded. The fear of annoying the husband of his pronouncing Talaq in relation of vengeful ouster by him factors like these choke the demanded. This point can be illustrated with the facts of a recent case E.V.Kuhimariam Vs. O.Mammu[18]. In words of Justice Sukumaran "This case may serve as a study in the continuing suffering of Indian womanhood. The legal battle for getting a partly amount of less then Rs.2000 by way of Mahr and past maintenance spanned a period of nearly a decade and spread over three courts including the High Court." The conclusion of this long story is like this. The defendant (M) was married, had six children and at the time of seventh, when his wife at her parents house, he married a young girl, the petitioner (K) in April 1976. In July when the first wife returned, he packed off (K), already pregnant, to her parents home and abandoned her and the child (M) was a rich man. When (K) filed a maintenance petition Under Section 125 Cr.P.C., (M.) in relation divorced her. He sent Rs.I05 as Mahr and Rs.200 towards past maintenance. (K) claimed Rs.2000 only as Mahr, but that was denied. So the legal battle ensured finally, the High Court decreed Rs.2000 as Mahr on the basis of the custom of the parties and Rs.60 and Rs.25 as maintenance amounts for the petitioner (K) and her child respectively. The right to dower is heritable. It vests in the heirs even if prompt dower is not demanded by the wife during her life time. After the termination of the marriage by divorced or otherwise there is no difference between prompt and deferred dower.

(b) Deferred Dower - Mahr - i - Muwajjal

The deferred dower becomes payable on the termination of marriage by death or divorce. It does not become prompt by the demand of the wife during the continuance of marriage. The liability to pay deferred dower binds the husband during his lifetime and his estates after his death. If the wife predeceases the husband the dower would become due at once and will not be postponed till the death of the husband, but if there is an agreement for payment of dower earlier than the dissolution of marriage such an agreement would be given effect to. The deferred dower cannot be demanded till it is due. But he husband may pay it off by transferring property in lieu therefore or may agree that even deferred dower may be recoverable on demand. The deferred dower is an unsecured debt. The secured creditors will not be prejudicially affected by any transfer affected by the husband in favour of his wife, in lieu of deferred dower. So far as the unsecured creditors are concerned it is always open to them to impugn such a transfer, according to the ordinary law of the land. It was held in Ghisuddin Babu Khan Vs. Commissioner of Income Tax,[19] that where a Muslim prefers one of his unsecured creditors and transfer all his properties to such creditors, the remedies which the other unsecured creditors have in such a situation, would dower equally by available in case of transfer in favour of a wife in lieu of deferred dower, no more, no loss. The nature of dower shall be prompt or deferred, it is primarily a matter of contract between the parties. Where there is such a contract, such portion of the dower as is agreed to be prompt shall be prompt and rest shall be deferred but in case where it has not been specified as to what portion is to be prompt, there has been a difference of opinion as to whether the whole of it should be presumed to be prompt or only a part. Mr. Macnaughten, on a consideration of the original authorities was of opinion that the whole should be presumed to be prompt while Baillie was of opinion that a portion should be held to be prompt with due regard to custom for the life of the woman. There is preponderance of opinions in favour of Baillie's conclusions. The Privy Council citing Mr. Macnaughten' s view as authoritative held that the whole dower should be presumed to be prompt but this was a Shia case[20] to which the law was correctly applied by the Privy Council. Ameer Ali[21] says that it is customary in India to fix one half (1/2) of the dower as prompt and the remaining moiety as deferred or postponed. This is said to have been the custom in India under the Moughal Emperor Aurangzeb. It has, however been held in Allahbad, Bombay, Patna and Lahore that only a reasonable proportion should be presumed to be prompt, regard being had to custom, status of the parties and the account of dower settled. Allahabad High Court declared in Eidan Vs. Mazhar Hussain[22] one fifth (l/5) of dower amount as prompt as the wife had been a prostitute, and in Taufikunnisa Vs. Ghulam Kambar[23] one third (1/3) held prompt. In Rehana Khatoon Vs. Iqtidaruddirr[24] out of Rs.12000 out of Rs.51000 held prompt and in Mst. Mainunnav.

Vs. Sharafatillah[25], half of the full dower amount held prompt. Bombay High Court in Fatima Bibi Vs. Sadrudin[26] held one third of the dower amount prompt this High Court has also held that the court has got the power to award even the whole amount as prompt in Hussein Khan Vs. Ghulab Khatoon[27]. The Madras High Court has however, held that if the character of dower is not specified to be prompt in the case of all Muslims at least in Madras Presidency.[28]

In Ithna Ashari law the presumption is that the whole of the dower is prompt. Tyyabjii[29] writes with the reference with a Full Bench decision that lays dower first that where the Kabinnama is silent on the question, the usage of the wife's family is the main consideration; and secondly, that is the absence of proof of custom, the presumption is that one half (1/2) is prompt and other half deferred and the proportion may be changed to suit particular cases.

Reference:-

1 The Quran, IV: Translated by Mr. Yusuf Ali

2 Ameer Ali - Mohammedan Law

3 Mst.Mahtabunnisa Vs. Rifaqatullah: AIR 1925 (All) 474: 85 IC. 459

4 Bashir Ali Vs. Hafiz Nazir: 4 IC 4 62

5 Mohammad Shahabuddin Vs, Mst.Umator Rasool : AIR 1960 (Pat.) 511

6 Ameer Ali-Mohammedan Law

7 Nujumooden Ahmed Vs. Beebee Hoosicnee: 4, Suth W.R. 110

8 Ekram Hussain Vs. Ali Hussain: 17 Pat. L.T. 423

9 Kulsambi Vs. Bilankhan : AIR 1929 (Nag.) 21

10 Zakeri Begum Vs. Sakina Begum: I.L.R 19 (Cal.) 686

11 Asma Bibi Vs. Abdul Samad: I.L.R. 3 (All.) 167: 5 I.C. 411

12 Sughra Vs. Masuma: I.L.R. 2 (All) 473 (FB)

13 Mst. Jaddo Begum Vs. Nawab Sharf Jehan Begum: AIR 1921 (Oudh) 194

14 Mst.Bibi Bachun Vs. Sheikh Hamid: 14 M.I.A. 377

15 Syed Sabir Hussain Vis. Farzand Hussain: 1937 (65) I.A. 119,127 Fat Law 669

16 Abdul Rahman Vs. Mst. Inayator: AIR 1937 (Oudh) 63

17 Marina Jalos Vs. Nuruddin Jatoi : P.L.O. 1967 (SC) 580

18 E.V. Kuhimariam Vs. O.Mammu : AIR 1985 (Ker) 239

19 Ghisuddin Babu Khan Vs Commissioner of Income Tax: A.P. III. Hyderabad 1985 Tax L.R. 1058 at P.1066 (A.P.)

20 Mirza Bedar Bukht Vs. Mirza Khurram Bukt : (1873) 19 W.R .315 D.C

21 Ameer Ali - Mohammedan Law

22 Eidan Vs. Mazhar Hussain: I.L.R.I (All) 483

23 Tautikunnisa Vs. Ghularn Kambar : I.R.R. I (All) 506

24 Rehana Khatoon Vs. lqtidaruddin : AIR 1943 (All) 184 P. 187

25 Mst. Mainunnav. Vs. Sharafatillah : AIR 1931 (All) 403: 29 A L.J. 197

26 Fatirna Bibi Vs. Sadrudin: (1865) 2 B.H.C. R 291.

27 Hussein Khan Vs. Ghulab Khatoon : I.L.R. 35 Born.386

28 Masltan Sahib Vs. Assam Bibi : I.L.R. 23 (Mad.) 371 [FB], Sheikh Mohd. Vs. Bibi : AIR 1938 (Mad.) 107

29 Tyabbji - Muslim Law

CHAPTER-V

CHAPTER-V
Quantum and Enforcement of the Mahr

1. Quantum of Mahr.
2. Factors determining the quantum of Mahr.
3. Increase or decrease of Mahr.
4. Enforcement of Mahr.

" .... all others,
Are lawful, provided,
Ye seek (them in marriage)
With gift from your property
Desiring chastity, not lust,
Seeing that ye derive,
Benefit from the, give them,
Their dower (at least),
As prescribed: but if,
If a dower is prescribed, ye agree,
Mutually (to vary it),
There is no blame on you,
And God is all knowing.
All wise.[1]

Under Islamic Law an adult wife has every right to deal with her Mahr in any way she likes. Prior to the Islam the dower amount which was generally paid or taken by the father of the bride was prohibited by the Islam and it was commanded by Almighty God that the right of dower is not the right of the father of the bride but it should be paid to the wife and not her father or other relatives. It is derived in the Holy Quran

Quantum of Mahr

There is not fixed rule as to the determination of the amount of dower. Normally dower is fixed by the mutual consent of parties before the solemnization of marriage. No particular process or any formal documentation is needed. Actually customs and usages determine these factors. Different sections of Islam followers their own rules relating to the amount of dower which is required under the law governing them. Apart from the nature of dower, legal controversies surround the question of dower amount, its bifurcation into prompt and deferred portions, the time and mode of payment, revision of dower and excessive dower. All these legal issues are hereinafter examined. An attempt is made to analyse the judicial precedent to find out and state the principles governing each of these areas.

However, the Indian courts do utilize the sectarian legal rules as regards the fixation of dower amount but normally they also take the help of legal principles of universal applicability. Further, besides equity, the most dominant legal norm which condition this branch of law is the Law of Contract. This is so because marriage is regarded as a civil contract in the Indian Law till to date. The principles which apply to civil contracts have profoundly shaped the law relating to marriage relationship in India.

As far as the Quantum of Mahr is concerned under Hanafi Law, the minimum limit of the dower amount is equivalent to 10 Dirhams and there is no upper limit. Where ever the dower is less then the minimum limit, then it must be made up to that amount. It is 10 Dirhams or an equivalent there of which has been unanimously accepted by the courts of India in limit concern with minimum amount of Mahr but there is no any general principle of universal application and uncertainty still exists so as the actual amount the courts may decree. In Shafi Law and Shite Law there is no provision for minimum amount for Mahr. But in Maliki Law minimum amount for Mahr is 3 Dirhams. The amount of Mahr may either fixed or not: if it is fixed it can not be a sum less than the minimum laid down by their particular law of different schools.

Value of 10 Dirhams

The quantum of the value of 10 Dirhams is matter of discussion and uncertainty. The value has not been finally decided. Amir Ali[2] says, its value is amount 5 shilling. Macnghten says, that the value of 10 Dirhams in Asma Bibi Vs. Abdul Jamal[3] is between Rs.3 and Rs 4. In Sughra Vs. Masuma.[4] It was decided that the value of 10 Dirhams is Rs. 107. In the decision of Mst. Jaddo Begum Vs. N awab Sharaf Begum[5], the value of 500 Dirhams was fixed at Rs.110. The value is still uncertain. But it is a silver coin containing 2.97 Grams of silver and the best course would be seem to be is to calculate the value according to price of silver of that quantity.

Maximum Dower

Where the law fixes a minimum limit for dower, there is no maximum limit is prescribed for dower whatever amount exceeding the minimum settled will be payable. In Shia Law also, according to better opinion there are no bounds to the quantity or value of dower. The moderation is commendable and fixing of Mahr (dower) exceeding Mahr-ul-Sunh (500 Dirhams) is considered to be abominable but not illegal. In Indian society of Muslims two distinct tendencies are to be found. In some cases, as in Sulaymani Bohras the dower is Rs. 40, it being considered a point of honour not be stipulate for a sum higher than the minimum fixed by the Holy Prophet Mohammad for his favorite daughter Fatima the wife of Ali, namely 500 Dirhams. In other communities, there are dowers of anything between Rs.100/- to Rs.1,000/- Ameer Ali[6] mentions amounts between Rs. 4/- to Rs. 4,000/-. An altogether different tendency is to be found in Uttar Pradesh and also to some extent in Hyderabad, Deccan where the absurd rule appears to be that the nobler the family, the higher the Mahr, regardless the husbands capacity to payor ability to earn.

Factors relating to determine the Mahr

Mahr is settled by the courts if the dower is not either settled or expressed in the documents at or before witness and opinions differ. The elements which are taken into consideration by the court in such cases have been discussed and expressed at length by the Patna High court through Mr. Justice B.N. Raichand & Mr. Justice S.C. Prasad in Mohd. Shahabuddin Vs. Mst. Umator Paroo[7]. The following observation made in this case express the considered view of the said court and in this quoted in extensor, as under:

"Such as the circumstances of the husband and the wife, the necessity of a device to prevent on the part of the husband the arbitrary exercise of the power of divorce vested in him, the position of paternal family of the woman her attainments or personal attractions and qualifications, wealth of her husband, condition of society surrounding her and the desire of self glorification and vanity on the part of the parties. All these considerations enter into the determination and settlement of the amount of dower. "

From the above observation in following conclusions are very much relevant for consideration:

(1) The circumstance of husband and wife;

(2) The necessity of a device to prevent on the part of the husband the arbitrary exercise of the power of divorce vested in him;

(3) The position and family pattern of the woman;

(4) Her intellectual attainment, personal attraction & her qualification;

(5) The wealth of her husband and condition of society surrounding her and

(6) The desire of self glorification and vanity on the part of the parties.

All these factors are relevant and prevalent in contemporary India. Now here it is necessary to mention that different circumstances of each case to a large extent influence the court in granting a particular amount of wealth as Mahr in favour of the wife. The certain rules judicially evolved for the purpose of determining the Mahr amount in normal case. These principles are as followed:

(l) The amount of Mahr may be calculated on the basis of analogy. The Mahr of her sister, paternal aunt or paternal parallel cousin cases. But for the application of this rule it is necessary that they should be more or less like the wife concerned with regard to age, beauty, virginity, education, financial status, character and the like;

(2) The Mahr of the girl of the same family if substantially unequal in respect of above qualities, will not be taken as a standard to fix the Mahr amount; and

(3) The Mahr of mother and of the other girls of her family will not be taken as a standard except where the mother is an agnatic relation.

In Abdul Rahman Vs. Inayat Bibi[8] It was opined that no hard and fast rule can be laid down as the determination of the amount of proper Mahr, the court is generally to be guided by three consideration:-

(1) The social position of the family of woman's father;

(2) Her own personal qualifications and

(3) Judiciary very cautiously took the view in Nujummoddon Ahmed Vs. Beebee Hoseinee[9] that in determining proper dower, with other consideration, the position of the husband must not be altogether excluded from consideration as unequal marriages are often take place.

Mahr-as-Sunuat.

Now, it is very necessary to discuss here, the concept of Mahr-asSunnat or Mahr Taljee, The meaning of Sunnat is 'sound' or 'fame' and 'infinitive of the verb be heard'. In many cases the parties settle privately a small amount for dower but merely for show and family pride a large sum is mentioned although the parties do not intend to payor exact such large amount. If the parties have really contracted for a high amount of made for a smaller sum and a bigger sum is given out simply for the purposes of show, and then the court will be entitled to reduce the amount to that actually settled as payable. The court can hold that such contract is sham and not real.

The onus of proving the fictitious nature of the dower is on the party making the allegation as to its fictitious nature. If the terms of a fictitious dower have been reduced to writing in the form of a deed, the question will arise whether the party setting up the fictitious nature of the dower is entitled to lead evidence as to its real nature and to prove that dower actually settled was not what was shown in the written marriage deed. Will it be barred by the provisions of Section 91 of the Indian Evidence Act? It is submitted that it will not be barred.

Increase or Decrease of Mahr

The husband may at any time after marriage increase the dower and a wife can remit the dower. Wholly a partially and a Muslim girl who has attained puberty is competent to relinquish her Mahr, although she may not have attained majority age of 18 years with the pursuit of the Indian Majority Act. The decisional law in India reflects the variable disputations which often arise in case of a controversy relating to the amount of dower, the court may decree in favour of the wife. The matter appears to be governed by local customs and the terms of the written marriage deed. As regards customs as Ameer Ali is of the view that among the upper middle class the minimum and maximum varied between Rs. 4,000/- to Rs. 40,000/-. In Bihar Rs. 40,000/- is the customary dower while in lower Bengal there is no custom. In lower classes in India, it varied Rs.50 to Rs. 400/-. In princely families, it usually consisted of several lakhs of rupees. Thus, according to this observation, in India upper middle classes and lower classes constituted two distinct groups. As regards the various reasons, he speaks of a uniform pattern while in Bengal he notes the non-existence of the custom relating to the amount of dower. Finally, he also pointed out that the princely family constitutes the distinct group so far as dower is concerned. It is clear that amount of dower proportionately increases or decreases with the variation of the financial status of various groups. Bihar constitutes a unique exception to this general rule as a single amount is generally the customary dower. As regards to the Bengal, no customary dower is the criterion and different scale of the dower amount is adopted by the families concerned according to circumstances of their home.

Where customary dower referable to a particular class of people exists, then it constitutes the dominant factor in the determination of the dower amount which could be or usually decreed by the courts. The real difficulty arises in those cases where neither a custom exists nor it is disclosed by the marriage deed. Another feature of this aspect of family relationships which requires notice is that speaking generally an amount disproportionate to the financial capacity of husband was often settled as dower. This tendency was taken notice of the Privy Council also in Zakiria Begum Vs. Sakina.[10] In Oudh and Jammu Kashmir regions in India presented a unique problem. In these areas many princely families and those of the erstwhile landed proprietors resided. They were reduced to a vary low financial status by the vessitude of times but still clung to their bygone status and provided themselves in various ways. One of the those ways was to fix an anormous amount of dower absolutely to disproportionate to the financial status of the husband. The result was that various hardships and injustices attended all those occasions when the amount so settled had to be paid. The problem assumed such proportions that the then Government found it necessary to intervene by way of legislation. The Oudh Laws Act, 1876 was passed wherein provided that where the stipulated dower was excessive as compared to the financial capacity of the husband, then the court was not obliged to decree such an amount of dower but only a reasonable amount with reference to the means of the husband. By way of ultra caution it was provided that excessive dower amount will not be decreed directly or indirectly, by allowing it by way of set-off, lieu or otherwise to the defendant.

In the world of regulatory legislation again and identical provision is found in Section 2 of the J & K state Muslim Dower Act, 1920. In both the places (Oudh and J & K) the provision is applicable only to the persons having a local domicile. In this context, the observation of the Privy Council is noteworthy. Lord Hannen (on behalf of Lord Macnaghton, Sir Richard Couch and Lord Shand) though the Privy Council held in Zakaria Begum's case as referred to that in case if a man resides outside Oudh province and goes to Oudh and marries there, the provision of the Oudh Laws Act, 1876 could not be invoked. The civil courts were thus directed to fix the reasonable amount of dower were stipulated dower was excessive. The courts thus, had to make to determinations:

(a) Whether the stipulated dower was excessive with reference to the means of the husband: In Sheik Abdur Rahman Vs. Sheik Wali Mohammad, the plaintiff s appeal deals only with the amount of dower. Section 5, Oudh Laws Act, lays down that where the amount of dower stipulated for in any contract by a Muslim and is found excessive with reference to the means of the husband, the holy amount mentioned in marriage deed shall not be awarded in any suit by decree in favour of the plaintiff or by allowing it by way of set-off, lien or otherwise to the defendant, but the amount of dower to be allowed by the Court, shall be reasonable with reference to the means of the husband.

(b) Where it was so, then the court was to make an honest calculation of the reasonable amount of dower and guiding principle was the same as applied in case of the former.

Obviously the discretion was to be exercised reasonably not arbitrarily either on its own or on the plea of the husband; once such a plea was forwarded it becomes obligatory for the court to decide the issue one way or another. What is to be specifically noticed is that the court was invested with the power to release the dower amount but had no corresponding power to increase it on these cases where the dower amount was ridiculously low having regard to the means of the husband.

It may be pointed out that after the commencement of the Constitution of India ensures equality before law and equal protection of law to all without any discrimination specially on the ground of sex, the provision of sections of the Oudh Laws Act, 1876 appears to be discriminatory. However, in British India the utility of referred legislation was acknowledged by Jurist and Judiciary in view of the prevailing conditions. The Judiciary while administering the said statutory provisions has not followed any hard and fast rule for determination of the reasonable dower and very rightly too.

The Oudh Chief Court in Sheikh Abdur Rahman V.3s. Sheikh Wali Mohammad[11] in 1931 declared that the principles for decreasing the amount of dower proved to have been settled between the parties could not be regulated by a pre-determined formula and the circumstances of the case particularly the statutory standard i.e. the means the husband shall determine the amount which the court may decree as dower. These enactments effectively eradicated the evils to which they were directed and thus remedied in the Islamic behavior on the part of the people domicile within the territorial boundaries of the areas to Oudh and J&K which they applied. These statutory measures to the extent of their application excluded the application of the principles of Muslim Law and Law of Contract affecting the disputes relating to the amount of dower and the payment thereof. But as regards rest areas (Others than Oudh and J&K) the legal position remains unchanged.

Two major principles relating to question of dower were adopted and applied by the courts in rest areas and for sake of clarify they may be noted down as follows:-

(a) Where a particular sum of money or property was proved to have been settled either through witnesses or the marriage deed or determined on the basis of substantial evidence like custom or Mehr-ul-Misl, then such amount was decreed irrespective of the financial capacity of the husband or the consequences arising out of the satisfaction of such decree. In short, once proved to have been settled, the dower amount was decreed notwithstanding any other consideration; and

(b) Where there was neither a written contact nor conclusive proof in form of testimony of witnesses, then dower of equal was a general rule taken as standard irrespective of the claims and rival claims of the parties.

One of the typical cases which represents the application of the first rule is Kulsambi Vs. Bilankhan[12] where it was observed that the excessive dower was often settled but is no case affect the validity of the claim of the wife. In this case, wife claimed and proved by the testimony of three witnesses that her dower was fixed at Rs.50,000/- plus 100 Ashafees and 50 Dinars. Her claim was accepted by the court even though there was no documentary evidence and it was prima facie excessive having regard to the means of the husband. Likewise the Lahore High Court in Mohd. Sultan Begum Vs. Sarajuddin

Ahmed[13] through Mr. Justice Agha Haider declared that the mere fact that amount of Mehr is beyond the husband's means would be no defence to wife's claim. Similarly the Rangoon High Court in Mohd. Ibrahim Vs. Ma Ma[14] held that, however, large the dower amount fixed may be the wife is entitled to recover the whole of it from her husband's estate without reference to his circumstances either at the time of marriage or the value of his estate at the time of his death. The second rule which is attributed to the observation of Syed Ameer Ali has been followed by the court and the case of Ekram Hussain Vs. Ali Hussain[15] may be taken as an example. It was held by the Patna High Court that in case of a dispute about the amount of dower where there existed no documentary proof or the testimony of witnesses about such fixation, the court will be guided by the statement of Syed Ameer Ali and the local customs. It was proved that the customary dower in Bihar was Rs.40,000/-. Secondly, the dower of the first wife of the defendant was also Rs.40,000/-. The court accepted these factors as decisive and decreed Rs.40,000/- as dower amount. Here it can be concluded the reasons which often weigh with the wife's family which normally tries to have a large dower amount fixed at the time of marriage in following times:

(a) to provide a counter to the unqualified right of divorce enjoyed in fact by the Muslim matter in India;

(b) to provide economic security to the girl as against unforeseen calamities like death, abandonment and divorce; &

(c) false sense of social superiority and the satisfaction of vanity and vain pride.

All these variable factors work with varying intensity in the determination of the dower amount. Further as the minimum is fixed by the Hanafi School with no upper limit & majority of Indians following this school feel free in this matter of fixation of dower. On the other hand, the followers of Shia School are more circumscribed in this matter because anything above the equivalent of 500 Dirhams is considered as unapproved or Makrooh (undesirable). Thus the problems remain both in case of marriages where dower is excessive (except in areas where the statutory law is applied) as well as where the amount is ridiculously low. As regards the former, the Muslim Jurists were well aware of the problems and Qazi had the authority to reduce excessive dowers in appropriate cases exercising the discretionary authorities according to the well-established norm of judicial behavior.

After having a glance on judicial trend regarding the excessive dower and its prevalence with numerous objections in India, researcher is under mandatory objection to look into the Islamic stand on amount of dower. It is mandatory obligation to look into the Islamic stand on amount of dower. If Islam's intention was that dower should serve as a financial security for 'rainy days' to woman, why does it say in the Revealed Book: -

And give the woman
(On marriage) their dower
As a free gift, but if they
Of their own good pleasure,

Remit any part of it to you,
Take it and enjoy it
With right good cheer.[16]

Now days, no doubt, the practice is generally that the dower has an aspect of a guarantee and an undertaking, that is, the man makes an agreement for a certain amount in the form of dower, but the woman does not generally demand it, except on the occasion of a difference or dispute that might arise between them. This kind of dower can transform itself into a security. In the early days of Islam, the practice was that the man used to give as a dower in money or in kind, anything that he undertook to part with. So in view of this fact it cannot be said that the object of Islam in ordering the dower was to provide woman with a financial security. The Islamic matrimonial history provides evidence that the Prophet Mohammed was never ready to hand over a woman to a man without the payment of the dower. An incident is reported with slight difference between the Shia and Sunni Authorities that a woman came to the Prophet Mohammed and stood before him saying "0 Prophet Mohammed in respect of the request of the woman kept silent and said nothing. The woman sat down in her place. One of his companions stood up and said, "0 Messenger of Allah, if you are not ready I am prepared to accept her as my wife.

The Prophet Mohammed asked: what would you submit as a dower? "I have not got anything was the reply. This cannot be, go to your house, perhaps you will find something there to give as a dower to his woman, the Prophet Mohammed said the man went to his house, came back and said, "I could not find anything in my house." The Prophet Mohammed said, "Go again and look well. If you can find a mattel ring even that would suffice" said the Prophet Mohammed. He went twice and came back and said, "I cannot find even a metal in my house. I am ready to present her with the clothes that I am wearing as her dower". Another one companion who knew the man, said: "0 Messenger of Allah, by Allah, this man has no other clothes except those he is wearing. So, the half of the clothes may be assigned as the dower of the woman. The Prophet Mohammed said: " if half of these clothes are to be the dower of the woman, who will wear which half? If one of them wears them, the other will remain undressed. No, it cannot be like this." The man who had made the request sat down. The woman also waited in her place. The gathering took up some other topic and the discussion lasted for a long time. The man who had requested the hand of the woman started to go away but the Holy Prophet Mohammed called him.

"Come over here" ! he came ..
"Speak, tell me, can you recite some of the Suras."
"Yes, I can."
Very good. Now it is all right.
So I marry this woman to you and
her dower will be that you teach her the Quran."
The man took the hand of the woman and went away.

Plea for Remission

Under the Islamic Law, dower is an incident of marriage which is backbone of the society. It is stated in the Holy Quran, "Seek them in marriage by gifts from your property", hence it is clear that the very inception of this relationship gives to the settlement of some property by the husband in favour of the wife.

The value of this settlement shall be proportionate to the financial status or means at the disposal of the husband. The general rule is that poor or wealthy, each according to one's means should settle some property in favour of the wife at the time of marriage. Moreover, the liability instead of miserness is the desired course indicated by the Divine Guidance in financial relations between the spouses. This settlement is treated as personal property of the wife and she can exercise all those rights which are enjoined to an absolute owner. Consequently, she can reduce or remit or make a gift of the whole or part to any person she may choose including the husband (even after his death) and the heirs of the husband. In case of remission of dower by way of gift, acceptance by the donee is not necessary, however, in cases where it is by way of sale, registration is legally required. Her rights are absolute and independent as regards the marriage settlement and a contract to the contrary i.e. she will not demand any amount as dower, is void in law. An adult wife has every right to deal with her dower in any way she likes, she can validly agree to; its reduction or remission or can make a gift of the whole or part of it to her husband or, after his death, to his heirs or to any other person. Such a gift can be conditional, and if it is made by a widow to a deceased husband or his heirs, it is treated as a release of the claim, which is effective without their assent. The covenant to release before marriage, or the covenant that she would not demand any amount as dower after marriage, is void in law, as dower is a necessary incident to marriage, but after the marriage has been celebrated, her rights are absolute and independent of any control of any agency.

Though the contract as to remission of Mahr is without consideration and the Quranic injunction in this regard permits that such contract is valid even without consideration but the free consent of the wife who is making remission is under lined, and thus the consent of the wife must be free and for example, if the remission is made by the wife while in great mental distress owing to her husband's death, it cannot be said to have been made with free consent and same is not binding on her. Acceptance of remission of Mahr by beneficiary is not essentially required. Thus remission of Mahr even after the husband's death is valid even without the acceptance of the husband's heirs and even if it is without consideration. It was the decision of Bombay High Court that it is not necessary to give importance to acceptance and consideration, but the free consent must be established in every such case.

The Calcutta High Court in Nurunnissa Khanum Vs. Khaja Mohammad Sakru[17] through Mr. Justice Choudahry and Mr. Justice Cuming observed that "where a Muslim lady, when overwhelmed with grief at the death of her husband, orally relinquished her right to dower on suggestion of her mother and sister - held that under circumstances of the case, there was no exercise of fee and deliberate judgment, and relinquishment made was invalid. This was a suit by the plaintiff Nurunnissa Khanum claiming Rs.15,000/- as dower due from the estate of her deceased husband Khaja Mohommed Arjoo, The defendant, who was the brother of the deceased contested the suit and urged mainly that as the plaintiff had given up the dower at the time of the funeral ceremony of her husband and she was not entitled to the claim made. The court of the first instance accepted the contention and dismissed the plaintiffs suit. Against this decision, the plaintiff appeared to the High Court and for the appellant, it was contented that the relinquishment is invalid as there was no exercise of the free will, the plaintiff was over whelmed with grief and acted on the promptings of her mother and sister. Relinquishment of dower is not a question of Mohammedan Law, it is governed by Indian Contract Act and the provisions of Section 25 should have been completed with. The dower debt being a charge on immovable property in possession of the plaintiff could not be extinguished by mere word of mouth. The respondent it was pleaded that there was no question raised in the court of the first instance as to want of consent or under ....influence the remission will not become invalid merely because the lady was naturally disconsolate and weeping, relinquishment of dower is a matter governed by the Mohammedan Law and not by the contract. The respondent in support took the assistance of leading authorities on Islamic Law. Baillie[18] says that" the gift of dower to a dead husband is valid on a favorable construction of the law." A foot-note adds "to release him from responsibility at date of judgment." In support monumental text-books were cited: Ameer Ali[19] in his Mohammedan Law says "A woman may release her dower to her deceased husband that is a widow is entitled to exonerate or discharge the estate of her deceased husband from the liability of her dower debt." In Wilson's Digest of Mohammedan Law the Judges find a new Section 47-A added as "The release of dower by a wife to husband is expressly sanctioned by the Quran[20] and is therefore not void for want of consideration." The passage in the Qurarr' runs thus: Give the woman their dower freely, but if they voluntarily remit unto you any part of it enjoy it with satisfaction with satisfaction. The same Surah is voluntarily translated by Radwell thus "Give woman their dowry freely; but if of themselves they give up ought thereof to you, then enjoy it satisfaction as convenient and profitable. This passage refers to remission of the dower to the husband in his life time. "Voluntarily in its ordinary sense means, freely, but if of themselves they give up ought thereof to you, then enjoy it as convenient and profitable. "Voluntarily in its ordinary sense means freely, without compulsion, not under any obligation.

This was the decision in Jyani Begum Vs. Umrav Begum[21] that: according to Mohammedan Law a dower is debt and its remission by a widow without acceptance by the heirs of the husband is effective according to Mohammedan Law the remission of a debt extinguishes and it is not necessary that there should be any acceptance of the remission on the part of the debtor ... on the other hand, that the formula pronounced - I have given up my dower for the sake of God and His Apostle' showed that remission was in the form of a Sadaka (religious gift) : that a gift according to the Mohammedan Law requires tender, acceptance and seisin........" The learned Judge accepted the view that according to Mohammedan Law debt remitted is a debt extinguished and that no acceptance is required. This was the question in Ali Bhunimsa Bibi Vs. Mohd. Fathia Uddin[22] as to whether the relinquishment of a dower was an act in the matter of the Mahr and protected by Section 2 of the Indian Majority Act is invalid under the Indian Contract Act. In this case it was decided that relinquishment of her right to Mahr by a Mohammedan woman who is a minor under Indian Majority Act is invalid under the Indian Contract Act.

Under the Islamic Law it is well established that the character of the obligation to pay the dower is a debt. The moment the dower is settled, it is enforceable as a debt. The dower becomes the property of the wife by the mere contract and she may therefore deal with or dispose of it before taking possession of the same. The dower is the right of the woman solely and hence she is empowered to give it up or relinquish it in the continuance of the contract. As the debt is enforceable under the Contact Act, it can also be released Under Section 63 of the Contract Act, but the question is whether the remission which is said to have been made in this case can be considered as binding upon the lady and irrevocable. The Judge expressed the view that in all such cases free assent must be established. It must be shown that the lady voluntarily and deliberately gave up her right. It is quite true that the members of the family to which she belonged knew the precept in the Quran, if it can be so called and she also knew of instances in her own family where dower had been given up and that it was looked upon as a meritorious act. But she was overwhelmed with grief at the time, the body was just about to be removed for burial and that very near relatives spoke to her about its being a meritorious act. She was surrounded by female relatives and it is very natural that the under those circumstances a very young woman was led to say something which was understood as a relinquishment of her dower debt without having considered the matter from her personal necessity point of view and under a sudden emotional impulse. If a document had been given by this lady at that time relinquishing her right in favour of the heir it would have been looked upon with disfavor and we think that an alleged verbal relinquishment under such circumstances ought not to be favoured. No consideration seems to be needed for such relinquishment but what we have to see is whether she had the opportunity of considering the matter when it is said she gave up her claim. She was in the presence of death and in great mental distress. She had no time for freedom of thought and action. She was prompted by others and was not free agent at the time.

The Patna High Court held in Mohd. Zabain Vs. Mst.Bibi Sahidan[23] though Mr. Justice Meredith that Section 130 of Transfer of Property Act applies to Muslim woman wishing to release her husband from the liability of the payment of dower debt and hence release will be valid and binding only if it is done by means of writing an instrument. Generally a contract for relinquishment of a right is not binding without some consideration but in the case of dower,

Mohammedan Law has given every adult wife the right to forego her dower, wholly or in part, without consideration, whether the marriage has been consummated or not. The question has to be decided by reference to Mohammedan Law on the subject of the extinction and transfer of debts.

The Calcutta High Court in one of its decision held that it is open to the wife to give up her dower at any time after marriage (but not before or at the time of marriage) as Mohammedan Law never requires that it should take place immediately after the husband's death acceptance by the or the heirs is not necessary.[24] However, if the husband refuses to accept it. it returns to the wife, a remission may be made conditionally[25].

Under the law there is no doubt that it was the defendant who set up a case of relinquishment to show that the relinquishment was made by the lady voluntarily and of her own free without any pressure of any kind. It must to show that the lady had full opportunity of considering the matter when she gave up her claim. A relinquishment made at a time when the wife is great mental distress owing to her husband's death or is seriously ill will not be binding on her[26] .

The judiciary has given much emphasis on the point of age of female regarding to remission. The question is whether majority for purpose of relinquishment of dower is to be determined by Mohammedan Law or by the Majority Act. It has been held by Madras and Patna High Court that a remission made by a wife who has not attained majority under the Indian Majority Act, 1875, is invalid, though she may have attained majority by Muslim Law. The

High Court of Allahabad has dissented from this view and held that since the Section 2 of Indian Majority Act does not affect the capacity of any person "to act in the matter of marriage or dower[27], a Muslim girl who has attained puberty under Muslim Law is competent to relinquish her dower, though she may not have attained the age of majority (18 years) within the meaning of the Indian Majority Act.' The Allahabad High Court's view is correct as same is consonance to Islamic Law.

It is humble submission that the opinion of the different High Courts supporting the validity of remission of dower on the part of Muslim female provided competent under different statutory provisions e.g. Indian Majority Act and Indian Contract Act instead of applying the true principle of Islamic Law to determine the validity of remission is objectionable and such opinions deserve re-examination and correction in view of the provision of Section 2 of Muslim Personal Law (Shariat) Application Act, 1937 which ensures the protection of Muslim Personal Law and the matter of dower definitely constitutes the part of it and says that" Notwithstanding any custom or usage to the contrary in all question regarding Marriage, Dissolution of Marriage including Talaq, Ila, Zihar, Lien, Khula, Mubarat, Maintenance, Dower, Guardianship, Gifts, Trusts the rule of decision in case where the parties are Muslim shall be the Muslim Personal Law (Shariat), 1937.

The right of remission is recognized by Sura-Guidance[28] the permanent source of Shariat.

And give the women.

(on marriage) their dower
As a free gift; but if they
Of their own good pleasure,
Remit any part of it to you,
Take it and enjoy it
With right good cheer

Enforcement of the Mahr

And lawful for you are all woman besides those,
provided that you seek keen with your property, t
aking them in marriage, not committing fornication.
There as to those idom you profit (by marrying)
give them their dower as appointed.

Even the payment of dower is also necessary in the case of marriage with a slave girl. The Holy Quran says "so marry them with the permission of their masters and sue them their dower justly. It would appears from this that the Quran renders the payment of dower necessary at the time of marriage. The payment of dower was necessary even though it might be a very small sum. In exceptional case marriage is legal even though the amount of dower has not been specified at the time of Nikah, but it is obligatory and must be paid afterwards. Generally regarded as a consideration for the marriage, it is theory payable before consummation but the law allows its decision into two parts, one of which prompt payable before wife can be called upon to enter the conjugal domicile or demanded by the wife, the other deferred payable on the dissolution of contract by the death of either of the parties or by death. The specified or proper dower would be due to the following extent:

1. When full specified dower is due -
   (a) Where the marriage is valid and has been consummated or has been terminated by death ; or
   (b) Where the marriage is irregular, but has been consummated and specified dower is less than the proper dower.
2. One half of the specified dower is due where the marriage is valid and is dissolved before communication by divorce or apostasy or any other Act of the husband. If a valid marriage is dissolved on the ground of impotency without valid retirement the wife would be entitled to one half of the dower. But his would not be so if the marriage is cancelled in exercise of the option of puberty. But if the divorce results from any act of the wife of instance her apostasy or kissing the husband's son with desire or exercising the option of puberty before consummation, she would be entitled to no dower.
3. Proper dower - it is due in the cases specified in the section where the marriage has been consummated or dissolved by death provided that in the case of an irregular marriage, proper dower is less than the specified dower.
4. A present - It is due in the case of a valid marriage which is dissolved before consummation (except under an option of repudiation or by any misconduct of the wife) and the dower has not been specified at the time of the marriage. A present is

thus due in the same cases in which one-half of the dower should have been payable: if the dower had been specified at the time of the marriage. If, however, the dower is specified after the marriage and the marriage is dissolved before consummation, the wife would be entitled only to a present and not one-half of the dower subsequently specified.

In Shia Law - The right to dower is established only by coition. If one of the parties dies before consummation and before dower has been specified neither dower nor any present would be due. But in the case of the dissolution of marriage by divorce before consummation, a present would be due. In Shafei Law - A present is incumbent on the husband in every case of separation.

5. No dower - No dower is due in the following cases -
   (a) where the marriage is valid and is dissolved in exercise of an option of repudiation;
   (b) where the marriage is irregular and has not been consummated;[29]
   (c) where it has been dissolved by anything on the part of the wife (apostasy, adultery, etc.) before consummation;
   (d) where the marriage is brought about by force or by playing a fraud on the husband.[30]

A controversial legal issue is related to the question as to how much of the dower amount may be treated as prompt for deferred in a case. Where the parties to a marriage alliance did not finally decide about the quantum of the dower that how much of dower is prompt and what parts of it is deferred, the Shia Law holds that the whole of dower is prompt the Shia Law however, hold that only a part is prompt that how much of dower is prompt and what parts of it is deferred, the Shia Law holds that the whole dower is prompt, the Sunni Law however, holds that only a part is prompt. This part is to be fixed with reference to:

(i) custom;

(ii) the status of the parties; and

(iii) the amount of settled dower.

The judicial decisions in respect of Muslims belonging the Hanafi school has considered this question at length and some of more significant pronouncements are follows:

The Allahabad High Court in Abdul Kadir Vs. Salima[31] as back as 1886 expressed the view that the whole of the dower amount may be treated as prompt and payable either at the very first meeting of the spouses or on demand. The Bombay High Court in Hussain Khan Vs. Gulab[32] agreed with the view expressed by Allahabad High Court in a case which was considered by the court as back as 1911 on the contrary, the Madras High Court took the view in Sheikh Mohammad Rowther Vs. Aiyesa Bibi[33] that the whole of the dower amount must be regarded as prompt.

The Allahabad High Court in Mohammad Subhanallah Vs. Saghirunnisa[34] changed is old view and declared that in the absence of the evidence to the contrary only a past of the dower will be treated prompt.

The High Courts of Allahabad[35], Bombay[36] and Patna[37] held the view that in the absence of a proof to the contrary, the total dower amount shall be divided into two and proportion there of shall be determined according to the dictates of the usage or status of the parties in that order.

Following the above principle, the courts have shown once again a tendency to differ in this decision of the dower and on one occasion 1/5th and on other 1/3 rd of the total amount was treated as prompt but the Lahore High Court in Nasir-ud-Din Shah Vs. Amatul Mughni[38] laid a rule which is more reasonable and just having regard to the peculiar nature of marriage relationships. The correct emphasis that in the absence of usages, the equitable principles of equality shall apply and half of the dower will be treated as prompt while the other half will be taken as deferred. The payment of dower in every case neither at once nor deferred in every situation and for this very purpose, the law permits the decision of dower into two parts : prompt and deferred. The payment of prompt dower becomes due as soon as the marriage knot becomes complete and is payable on the demand of the wife. For the payment of prompt dower, wife is entitled to claim at any time, her previous demand and its refusal is not mandatory for the maintainability of the suit. She is entitled to recover her prompt dower at any time before or after the consummation. The Consummation has not the effect of converting the prompt dower into deferred dower. In short, prompt dower is payable immediately on the marriage taking place and it must be paid on demand. The right of the wife to prompt dower is not dependent upon consummation of marriage and suit for recovery of prompt dower is not premature for the want of consummation; for the payment of prompt dower wife is legally competent to refuse all conjugal rights of the husband till it is paid. The Peshawar High Court through Mr. Justice Mir Ahmad held in Mst. Pukhraj Begum Vs. Hidayat Ali Shah[39] that a wife can claim prompt dower before consummation of marriage.

In terms of time, the deferred dower becomes payable in view of the Lahore High Court in Sarb Krishan Vs. Mst.Fatima[40] on the termination of marriage by death or divorce. It does not become prompt by demand of the wife during the continuance of marriage-tie. The liability to pay deferred dower binds the husband during his life time and his estates after his death. If the wife predeceases the husband, the dower would become due at once and will not be deferred till the death of the husband but if there is an agreement for payment of dower earlier than the dissolution of marriage such an agreement would be given effect to. The deferred dower cannot be demanded till it becomes due, but the husband may pay it off by transferring property in lieu thereof or may agree that even deferred dower may be recoverable on demand.

Death of Either Party and Dower

If the marriage is dissolved by the death of either party even though by suicide dower shall be payable as:-

(1) In the case of a valid marriage full specified dower or if it has not been specified the proper dower whether the marriage has been consummated or not because by the death of the husband

or the wife, the marriage is rendered complete and every thing becomes established and confirmed by its completeness.

(2) In the case of a irregular marriage full specified or proper dower whichever is less, but only if it has been consummated but not otherwise. In Shia Law-if either party dies before consummation and no dower has been specified or agreed to be specified subsequently, or if it has been agreed that no dower shall be payable. Neither proper dower nor a present would be due and the proper dower is not established by virtue of the contract alone but is determined by its consummation. But if it has been agreed to be specified later, one-half of dower so specified will be due. But if marriage is dissolved otherwise than by death, a present would be due.

Result of Consummation on Dower

The marriage is consummated or not, this fact plays a very vital role in considering the amount of dower. The rights as to dower in consummated and unconsummated marriage would be different. The rights would be as follows:

(1) In the case of a consummated marriage, the dower will not be lost in any case (apostasy or other misconduct of the wife such as committing adultery or concealing illicit pregnancy or even the murder of the husband by her). The dower is confirmed and made binding by consummation (its substitute, valid retirement) just as by death. It will always be due as follows:

(a) In case of a valid marriage - full specified dower c proper dower if it has not been specified;

(b) In the case of an irregular marriage - full specifie dower or proper dower whichever is less.

(2) In the case of an unconsummated marriage, the dower shall b due only in the case of a valid marriage as follows:

(a) Where it is dissolved by death - full specifie dower or proper dower if it has not been specified.

(b) Where it is dissolved by divorce or apostasy or an other act of the husband - one-half of the specified dower if has been specified, otherwise a present.

Result of Unconsummated Marriage on Dower

No dower shall be due in the following cases if the marriage i unconsummated :

(1) Where the marriage is valid and has been dissolved:

(a) by the husband or the wife is exercise of an option c repudiation or

(b) for an act of the wife as her apostasy or adultery or

(2) Where the marriage is irregular.

Valid Retirement and Dower

When the husband and wife are all alone together unde circumstances as which present no legal moral or physica impediment to marital intercourses, they are said to be in vali retirement. The Raddul-Mukhtar lies down those four conditions are necessary: -

(a) there must be actual privacy ;

(b) there must not be any physical ,

(c) moral; &

(d) legal bar.

The valid retirement has the same legal effect as actual consummation in :

(a) Confirmation of Mahr.

(b) Establishment of Paternity.

(c) Observance of Iddat.

(d) The wife's right of maintenance and residence during Iddat.

(e) The bar of marriage with the wife's sister.

The valid retirement is not recognized under the Shia Law the right of dower is established by actual coalition either natural or against nature but not by mere retirement. The Shia Law, however. recognizes Tamkin-ul-Kamil which means such retirement as offers no impediment to conjugal relationship. It is analogous to Khilwat-us-Sahih of the Hanafis in some of its consequences. It entitles the wife to the right to maintenance where the question of consummation arises the fact will have to be proved and cannot be presumed as in the Hanafi Law. It has the same effect as consummation for eligibility of dower.

In Shia Law., the consummation alone or any act of familiarity, but not mere valid retirement effectuates the contract of dower.

Results of Apostasy on Dower

The apostasy from in the Islam of either party after consummation would not effect the eligibility of dower. It would be due in every case. But if before consummation, the husband apostatises, one half of the dower if it is specified, otherwise a present would be due but if the wife apostatises nothing would be due.

When Dower is Specified after Marriage

The whole of it would be payable of the marriage is consummated or terminated by death. If however, it is terminated by divorce, before consummation, only present would be payable according to Abu Hanifa and Mohammad. According to Abu Yusuf one-half of the dower would be due. In Shia Law - where dower is settled after marriage between the parties, it is called Mahr-i- Tafwij and when settled by arbitrators or judge it is called Mahr-i- Takhim. Where marriage is dissolved before consummation any dower settled as Mahar-i- Tafwiz or Mahr-i-Takhirn, one half of it will be payable to her.

Additions to Specified Dower

Additions to dower may be made at any time after marriage. In the case of valid marriage when it is dissolved after consummation or by death, such specified dower becomes due and such additions from part of the specified dower. Where however only one-half of the specified dower is due, one-half only of the original dower and not the addition will be payable. Thus in the case of an unconsummated marriage, additions would be void. If therefore no dower is fixed before or at the time of marriage but it is fixed after that, the wife would be entitled only to a present according to Abu Yusuf, additions would also form part of dower and one-half if it would be payable.

Unlawful Dower

When a dower is fixed which is party lawful the unlawful portion will be thrown entirely out of account. In which case, the wife would be entitled only to the lawful portion and not to proper dower. According to Hedaya, if the entire dower is unlawful, the wife would be entitled to proper dower.

When Dower is not Fixed

If at the time of marriage there is no mention of specific dower, proper dower would be payable where the marriage has been consummated or terminated by death.

Where Specified Dower is not Proper Subject of Dower

In all cases in which the specified dower is not valid dower. The proper dower would be recoverable, so in the case of contract of reciprocal marriage (Nikahi-i-Shighar) or where the dower is the rendering or sen/ices or the teaching of Quran. The wife would be entitled to her proper dower. If however a false assignment is made there is a difference of opinions. If for instance, the dower fixed is a cask of vinegar and it is found afterwards that it contains wine, the wife should be entitled to proper dower according to Abu Hanifa but according to Abu Yusuf and Imam Mohammad, she would be entitled to receive the same quantity of vinegar of medium quality. In Shia Law in this case the better opinion agrees with that of Abu Yusuf and Imam Mohammad.

Breach of Conditions

The parties to a marriage may make some conditions and they would be binding on them. If the husband makes a breach of such conditions, the wife would be entitled to recover her proper dower, if it exceeds the specified dower. Thus, if the husband has a stipulation made in the contract of marriage that he would not carry the wife out of her native city or that he would not marry any other woman during the subsistence of the marriage and commits a breach of such condition, the wife would be entitled to recover her proper if it exceeds the specified dower as it is advantageous to her.

Irregular Marriage

The Proper dower is payable in irregular marriage. In Shia Law, in all cases of void marriage which have been consummated, the wife is entitled to proper and not specified dower, if it is less than the specified dower.

Agreement against Dower

An agreement that no dower shall be payable is void and the wife is entitled to recover dower. In Ithna Ashari Law, the wife may, if she is adult, and of sound mind, agree not to receive any dower, the husband may receive an option to cancel dower. In Shafei Law, an agreement against dower made by a guardian on being asked by a woman of sufficient intelligence would be valid and if the husband dies before consummation nothing would be due. But if the marriage is consummated, the wife would be entitled to her proper dower.

Reference:-

1 The Quran - IV, 24. Translated by Mr. Yusuf Ali

2 Amir Ali - The Personal Law of Mohammedans

3 Asma Bibi Vs. Abdul Jamal: I.L.R (All) i.c. (44) 167: 5

4 Sughra Vs. Masuma: I.L.R. 2 All 473 F.B.

5 Mst.Jaddo Begum Vs. Nawab SharafBegum: AIR 1921 Oudh 194

6 Amir Ali - The Personal Law of Mohammedans

7 Mohd. Shahabuddin Vs. Mst.Umator Paroo : AIR 1960511 ; !.L.R. 38 (Pat) 624

8 Abdul Rahman Vs. Inayat Bibi : 7, C.W.N. 1181

9 Nujummoddon Ahmed Vs. Beebee I-Ioseinec : 4, Suth W.R.I 10

10 Zakiria Begum Vs. Sakina : I.L.R.19 (Cal) 686

11 Abdur Rahman Vs. Sheikh Wali Mohammad: AIR 1923 (Pat) 72; 68 IC 601

12 Kulsambi Vs. Bilankhan : AIR 1929 (Nag) 121 : 117 I.C.220

13 Mohd. Sultan Begum Vs. Sarajuddin Ahmed: AIR 1936 (Lah) 183

14 Mohd. Ibrahim Vs. Ma Ma : 1939 (Rang) 28

15 Ekram Hussain Vs. Ali Hussain: 17 Pat. L.J. 423

16 The Quran - VI, 4 translated by Mr. Yusuf Ali

17 Nurunnissa Khanum Vs. Khaja Mohammad Sakru : I.L.R. (1920) 47 Cal 537

18 Baillie - Digest of Mohammadan Law

19 Ameer Ali - Mohammedan Law

20 The Quran IV - 4,Translated by Mr. Ameer Ali

21 Jyani Begum Vs. Umrav Begum: 1908 I.L.R. 32 (Bom) 612

22 Ali Bhunimsa Bibi Vs. Mohd. Fathia Uddin: 1918 (41) Mad.1026

23 Mohd. Zabain Vs. Mst.Bibi Sahidan: 1942 AIR (Pat) 217

24 Nurunnissa Khanam Vs Khaja Mohd. Sakru : I.L.R. (1920) 47 Cal 537

25 Mst.Khadija Begum Vs. Nisar Ahmed: AIR 1936 (Lah) 887 : 39 P.L.R. 52

26 Md. Mashhud Vis. Md. Anwar: 1 r.c. 403 ; 6 A.L.J. 503

27 Qasim Hussain Vis. Bibi Kaniz Sabina: AIR 1932 (All) 649

28 The Quran IV - 4, Translated by Mr. Yusuf Ali

29 Maliq Iftikhar Wali Vs. Sarwari Begum: AIR 1929 (All) 369

30 Abdul LatifVs. Niyaz Ahmad: I.L.R.31 (All) 343

31 Abdul Kadir Vs. Salima : 1886 (8) All 149

32 Hussain Khan Vs. Gulab : 1911 (35) 80m 386

33 Sheikh Mohammad Rowther Vs. Aiyesa Bibi : 1938 AIR (Mad) 107

34 Mohammad Subhanallah Vs. Saghirunnisa: 1911 (41) All 562

35 Rehana Khatoon Vs. Iqtidar : 1943 AIR (All) 184

36 Fatima Vs. Sader - ud - din: 1865 (2) B.H.C.R. 291

37 Mahboban Bibi Vs. Moh. Ammcr-ud-din: 1929 AIR (Pat) 207

38 Nasir-ud-Din Shah Vs. Amatul Mughni: 1948 (Lah) 135 (FB)

39 Mst.Pukhraj Begum Vs. Hidayat Ali Shah: 1931\ AIR (Peshawar) 72

40 Sarb Krishan Vs. Mst.Fatima: 1937 AIR (Lah) 859

CHAPTER-VI

CHAPTER-VI
Mahr as Unsecured Debt & Wife's Right of Retention

Mahr as unsecured debt and wife's right to retention it.

(a) Wife's right to recover Mahr;

(b) Mahr as unsecured debt: &

(c) Wife's right to retention of the property in lieu of Mahr.

O Mankind reverence,
Your Guardian-Lord,
Who created you,
From a single person,
Created of like nature,
His mate, and from there twain
Scattered (like feeds)
Countless men and women;
Reverence God, through whom,
Ye Demand your mutual (rights),
And (reverence) the wombs
(That before you) for God
ever watches over you.[1]
They ask the instruction concerning the women
Say God doth,
Instruct you about them
And (remember) what hath
Been rehearsed upto you

In the Book, concerning.
The orphans of women to whom,
Ye give not the portions
Prescribed and yet whom ye
Desire to marry as also
Concerning the children
Who are weak and oppressed;
That ye stand firm for justice to orphans
There is not good deed
Which ye do, but God
Is well acquainted therewith[2].

The Quran clearly indicates that marriage is sharing between the two halves of the society, and that its objectives besides perpetuating human life are emotional well-being and spiritual harmony. Its bases are love and mercy. Besides all other provisions for her protection at the time of marriage it was specifically decreed that woman has the full right to her Mahr. In the previous chapter of this thesis, the researcher has tried to prove that the concept of Mahr in Islam is neither an actual or symbolic price for the woman but rather it is a gift symbolizing love and affection. The rules for married life in Islam are clear and in harmony with upright human nature. In consideration of the physiological and psychological make-up of man and woman both have equal rights and claims on one other. The Mahr is a woman's right and she can use it in whatever way the wants. No one can take it away from her. In Fatwa-i-Qazi Khan[3] says that Mahr is so necessary to marriage that if it is not mentioned at the time of marriage or in the contract itself: the law will presume it by virtue of the contract itself.

The Mahr is not merely a necessary incident or bride price, it is more than this. Virtually Mahr is an expression of love that is offered by the bridegroom to the bride. The author of Hedaya says "The payment of the Mahr is enjoined by the law, merely as a token of respect for the bride but the mention of it is not absolutely essential for the validity of a marriage and for the same reason marriage is also valid. It is designated by Sure-Guidance that the marriage relationship is above all monetary considerations and Mahr in fact is in the nature of a free gift. The reason of its importance lies in the protection that if it imparts to the wife against the arbitrary exercise of the power of divorce by husband. A Muslim husband can divorce his wife at his will and so the object of Mahr to check upon the capricious exercise of the husband of this power to terminate the marriage at will. It is not only protects her from his unbridle power to divorce but also from his extravagance in having more than wife. A stipulation to charge a huge Mahr on the occasion of his another marriage is enough to deter him from enjoying the luxury of having two, three, four wives.

Justice Mahmood has observed in Abdul Qadir Vs. Salima, that the marriage contract is easily dissoluble and freedom of divorce and the rule of polygamy place power in the hands of the husband which the law giver intended to restrain by rendering the rule as to payment of Mahr. That is why the right of the wife to her dower is fundamental feature of the marriage contract, it has a pivotal place in the scheme of the domestic relation affecting the mutual rights of the spouses at more than one point.

In this chapter firstly, the researcher will discuss the right of Muslim wife to recover her Mahr then after Mahr will discussed as un secured debt and the right of retention will also be discussed later on.

(a) Wife's Right to Recover Mahr

As far as wife's right is concern it depends on the nature of Mahr. As the researcher has already mentioned the different kinds of Mahr in earlier pages. If the Mahr is a prompt dower and it is still unpaid, the wife may refuse.

(i) to live with the husband; and

(ii) to admit him to sexual intercourse, if the marriage has not been consummated she has a right to refuse to cohabit with him as long as the prompt dower is not paid.

In the case of a wife who is minor or insane, her guardian has right to refuse to send her to her husband's house till payment of dower.

During her such a stay in her guardian's house the husband is bound to maintain her.[4] In this case it was held that the absolute right of the wife to insist on payment of the prompt dower before giving him the access to her is lost after the consummation. But if the question is arise whether the wife is entitled to refuse conjugal intercourse after consummation, there is a difference of opinion among the original authorities as also in the decision of the different High Courts. In the view of Imam Mohammad and Abu Yusuf a wife can not take the plea of non payment of Mahr if the consummation has taken place with her consent. But, if the consummation had taken place against her will or in condition when she was very young or insane she can take the plea of non payment of Mahr in a case of restitution of conjugal rights against her. Abu Hanafi's view in this matter is this that she is entitled to refuse conjugal intercourse even though the marriage had already been consummated. There is no absolute right in a husband to claim restitution of conjugal right against his wife unconditionally. In Rabia Khatoon Vs. Mukhtar Ahmed[5] the court declared that if the suit is brought after sexual intercourse has taken place with the free consent the proper decree that has to pass is not a decree of dismissal, but a decree for restitution conditional payment of prompt dower. If the nature of Mahr is deferred and if payable at a future date the courts have discretion to make the decree conditional on the payment of her unpaid dower debt or in impose other suitable condition considered just, fair and necessary in the circumstances of the each case. In Syed Ahmed Khan Vs. Smt. Imrat Jahan Begum[6], it was decided that where wife already have a decree in her favour for recovery of her prompt dower, and the husband was not paying it and in equity, the court ought to have made the satisfaction of the decree for recovery of dower as a condition for enforcement of the decree for restitution of conjugal rights.

The vital question which arose for consideration in the Full Bench case of Abdul Kadir Vs. Salima[7] was whether a Muslim wife has a right to refuse to go to her husband if her prompt Mahr is not paid even though the marriage had been consummated with the consent of the wife before the date of refusal. In this decision Justice Mahmood, whose judgment was adopted by the Full Bench observed that "The right of dower does not precede the right of cohabitation, or on the contingency of an event and there is no other contract to the contrary, the question is whether she can refuse to the husband, his conjugal rights or whether her guardian can detain her till payment?" In a suit by the husband to enforce his conjugal rights, the wife was entitled to refuse to cohabit with him, until he had paid which the contract of marriage necessarily involves, but that the two rights come into existence. "Simultaneously, by reason of the same incident of law. The right of the wife to claim maintenance from her husband arises in the same manner as one of the legal effects of the marriage, and may that any of those effects are not simultaneously created by the contract of marriage amounts, in my opinion, to a violation of the fundamental notion of jurisprudence regarding correlative rights and obligations arising from one and the same perfected legal relation."

After referring a passage in the Hedaya to make his point Mahmood J. expressed that Mohammedan Law entitles the wife to resist the claim of the husband for cohabitation with her by pleading non-payment of her prompt Mahr but is proceeds essentially upon the assumption that his right to put forward such a claim is antecedent to the plea. The same is the effect of the passage from "Darrual Mukhtar" and the view expressed in the "Fatwa Qazi Khan" and the "Fatwa-i-Alarngir Mahmood J. went on to say that the opinion of Imam Abu Hanifa to the contrary was not shared by his two eminent disciples Qazi Abu Hanifa and Iman Mohammad so far as the question of cohabitation was concerned and said that "Whenever there is a difference of opinion, of the two will prevail against the opinion of the third. Now bearing this in mind it is clear that the two disciples of Abu Hanifa, regarding the surrender of the wife to her husband as bearing analogy to delivery of goods in sale held that the lien of the wife for her dower as a plea for resisting cohabitation according to the ordinary rule of interpreting Mohammedan law, I adopt the opinion of the two disciples as representing the majority of the three Masters' and hold that after consummation of marriage non-payment of dower, even though eligible can not be pleaded in defense of an action for restitution of conjugal rights, the rule so laid down having of course, no effect, upon the rights of the wife to claim her dower in a separate action." Justice Mahmood. expressed his view that whenever there is a difference of opinion between Imam Abu Hanifa, the Master, and his two disciples Imam Mohammad and Qazi Abu Yusuf, the opinion of the latter must prevail over that of the former.

Mst. Anis Begum's case[8] was a another case in which the point for decision was this "whether the suit of husband for restitution of conjugal rights was liable to be dismissed on the ground that prompt dower had remained unpaid even though the marriage had been consummated with the consent of the wife prior to the refusal of the wife to live with the husband. On this point, Sir Suleman delivering the judgment of the Division Bench followed the view expressed by Justice Mahmood in Abdul Kadir Vs. Salima[9] and observed that "the two considerations which might well justify the acceptance of the view of the disciples in India, are first that, owing to the prevalent practice the amounts of dower fixed in this country are often unduly high and beyond the means of the husband. To allow to the wife the right of refusing to live with her husband, even after consummation so long as any part of the prompt dower remains unpaid would in many cases, where the husband and the wife quarrel, amount to an absolute option of the wife to refuse to live with her husband and yet demand a maintenance allowance. This will dislocate domestic life. Secondly as will be known here in after, under the Anglo-Mohammedan Law as administered in this country a suit for restitution of conjugal rights through brought for the enforcement of a right under the Mohammedan Law, is in the nature of the suit for specific performance and there is accordingly a certain amount of discretion in the count of justice which can impose a condition of previous payment of the dower debt or at, any rate a portion of it, in the decree." It was held by Learned C.J. in the decision that there was no right in the wife to refuse to return the husband after the marriage had been consummated on the ground that her dower had remain unpaid.

According to one School of Mohammedan Law, a Muslim wife governed by Hanafi Law has the right to refuse to so to her husband even after the consummation of marriage with the consent, if her dower remains unpaid. But it may be dangerous to adopt his view at the pleasant time and in the modern condition of the life. As it was pointed out by Sir Suleman J. the courts of law, have certain discretion in this matter because a suit for restitution of conjugal rights is in the nature of a suit for specific performance and it is open to the court to impose conditions on the husband to ensure the right of the wife to secure her prompt dower. According to Abu Hanifa, the deferred dower payable after definite term, the wife can not deny herself for the purpose of obtaining payment of dower either before or at the term. In the Shia Law the most favoured view of the scholar's of this school in regard is that the wife is not entitled to refuse conjugal intercourse for payment of prompt dower if marriage has already been consummated.

(b) Mahr as Unsecured Debt

The place of Mahr in the field of marriage relationship is very essential. This aspect of Mahr was discussed with a great importance in Hamira Biba Vs. Zubaida[10] "And it stood on the footing of being an ordinary debt and when the widow was in possession in right of her dower, the whole foundation of her right as against the heirs was as being creditor and she was entitled to amount as the dower-debt ranks at least equally with other debt, there is no doubt and the wife is entitled along with other creditors to have it satisfied on the death of the husband out of his estate. Her right, however, is no greater than that of any other unsecured creditor except that if she lawfully, with the express or implied consent of the husband or his other heirs obtains possessions of the whole or any part of his estate, she is entitled to retain such possession until her claim is satisfied, When a widow is then in the absence of an understanding she will be entitled to receive compensation of her exertion in the maintenance thereof on equitable considerations commonly recognized in the court of chancery are not foreign to Muslims system but are in fact often referred to and invoked in the adjudication of the cases."

The Lahore High Court in Mst. Nasiban Bi Vs. Mst. Iqbal Begum[11] through Mr. Justice Din Mohammad laid down that the dower amount can be fixed at any time before or after marriage and can also be increased during the continuance of marriage and where the husband promised to increase the dower was accepted by the wife, then the payment came to be binding on the part of the husband. The court referred with approval lahurdan Vs. Sakina Bibi[12] and Kamarunnissa Bibi's[13] case to the same effect or the observations of the pronouncements of acting Chief Justice Wazir Hasan (as then he was) and Mr. Justice Pullan in Mst. Amina Bibi[14] case. The Madras High Court in Abi Dhunimsa Bibi[15] laid down a proposition of far-reaching consequences reflecting the true nature of dower. "Courts never took at it (dower) from the point of view of mere consideration and regard it as an obligation enjoined on the husband by the marriage contract."

An analysis of the above discussed judicial decision reveals that dower is not consideration but a necessary incidence of marriage. Its existence or non-existence does not affect the validity of marriage. It may be fixed either before or after the marriage. The claim may be abandoned or reduced in value by the wire at any time during the continuance of marriage. The payment of dower is a charge over the estate of the husband. But it does not take precedence over other debts. However, if possession of estate is validly obtained by the wife, then she can retain the same so long as her claim remains unsatisfied.

In this sense she has the better claim than the other heirs the property of the deceased husband. The another aspect of wife's right to Mahr is that which the Madras High Court declared in Abi Dhunissia Bibi Vs. Mohammad Fathi-ud-din declared that the right to dower debt is heritable and transferable and may also be recovered from the heirs of the decreed husband. Mr.Justice Sashgiri Ayyar held that "the character of the objection to pay the dower is a debt. The moment the dower is settled to possess from precept into a enforceable debt the widow's claim for dower due from the estate of her decreed husband remarks equally and suitably with the claim of other creditors."

It is very well settled principle of Muslim Law and all the prominent scholars are agreed on this point that Mahr is an obligation imposed upon the husband as a mark of respect to the wife. The Mahr can be recovered by the wife by instituting an action in law as if it was a debt due to her. The obligation to pay Mahr to his wife gives rise to a debt in favour of wife. According to Muslim Law a Mahr can be prompt and of deferred. If it is deferred it is to be discharged when the specified event occurs and on demand made by the wife.

Mahr as a Debt

The Mahr of a Muslim woman is like any other debt and ranks pari passu with the claim of other creditors. Like any other creditors she can also institute a suit for her dower and she is also capable to obtain a decree against the assets of her husband. The Mahr is debt within the meaning of Indian Succession Act. In Amir Hasan Vs.

Mohd. Nasir Hasan[16] it was declared that even the wife's owns share is also proportionately liable for the satisfaction of her debt.

In Sughra Balbi Vs. Gaya Prasad,[17] it has been held that the deferred dower is incapable of being fairly estimated and if the husband becomes on insolvent it should not be entered in the schedule of creditor and the discharge of the insolvent should not be suspended on account of it. But a contrary view has been adopted in Bibi Janbi Vs. Abbas Ali[18] that interest in deferred dower is a vested and not a contingent one. It is not liable to be displaced by the happening of any event, not even her own death because her heirs can claim the money if she dies and it is a debt with in the meaning of Section 9 (1) (b) of the Provisional Insolvency Act.

Mahr not a Secured Debt

But, here it is important to mention, that although the wife ranks equally with other creditors her right is not greater than that if any other unsecured creditors. She is not entitled to any priority over other creditors she is not a secured creditors. Her claim for dower is a simple money claim and though the decree may be executed against the husband's property it can not be charged against any specific portion thereof. In Mst. Ahwadi Vs. Abdullah[19], it was declared that the court would not ordinarily created a charge on any property while passing a decree for dower because to such decree is to give dower debt a priority over others debts due from the husband. The court can properly pass only a simple money decree. A decree creating a charge would be set aside on appeal. But if the court actually passes a decree for a charge and the decree becomes final between the parties a chare would be created. The decree would not be a nullity for want of jurisdiction. A charge may be created by agreement. A decree for dower obtained by the widow of a Muslim against the other heirs even though it may be realizable from the assets of the decreed dower not create a chare against there assets.

In Abdul Rahman Khan Vs. Inyati Bibi,[20] It was held that a Muslim woman's claim for dower is a simple money claim though that decree may be executed against the husband's property.

Dower Payable before Distribution of Assets

As like any other debt Mahr being a debt has priority over inheritance and legacies. Like every other debt, dower must be paid before the heirs are entitled to take anything. It is a debt chargeable against the general estate of the deceased husband. The dower is due from the whole estate. Both portable and importable properties are liable for it. If, therefore, one of the heirs brings a suit for a share of the estate, the widow may, if she is a party, set up her claim for dower. Dower debt is a single debt and a succession certificate cannot be granted for recovery of a portion only.[21]

Heir's Right to sue for Share

Any heir may bring a suit to claim his own share in the estate of the husband but the wife may set up her claim for Mahr in such suit.

Heir's Right of Alienation

The heirs of a deceased Muslim is entitled to alienate their shares in the property even if the dower, which is like any other debt, remains unpaid. The right of enforcing the claim will of course be available to the widow and she will also be entitled to retain possession against unsecured creditors if she is already in possession.

Mahr as an Actionable Claim

There is nothing to prevent a widow from instituting a suit for her dower for the purpose of obtaining a simple money decree against all the assets of her husband including the property in her possession at least by surrendering possession of such property in her hands and it forbids a legal practitioner among other to buy any actionable claim. It can be taken in execution of a decree like any other debt. It does not fall within the exception assignable property created by Section6 (e) of the Transfer of Property Act, 1882.

Right to Mahr Transferable & Heritable

The nature of this right is heritable and the heirs are entitled to claim it even if the dower has not been demanded by the wife in her lifetime. The right is not lost even if the wife commits suicide before consummation contrary to the case of apostasy before consummation. If both the husband and the wife die, the heirs of the wife can claim from the heirs of the husband according to all, if the dower is specified but with respect to proper dower there is a difference of opinions, it would be recoverable according to Abu Yusuf and

Mohammad but not according to Abu Hanifa. The right is also transferable one. The wife may assign it to anyone. This is so in the case of deferred dower also and the transferee may recover it on its becoming due form the husband or his estate.

Failure to Claim Mahr under the U. P. Encumbered Estates Act.

If the husband files an application under the U.P. Encumbered Estes Act and there has been no demand by the wife and refusal by the husband, in respect of the prompt dower the failure of the wife to make a claim for it would not extinguish the debt Under Section 13 of the Act.

Discharge and Satisfaction of Mahr Debt

A Muslim wife's claim for Mahr may be satisfied in the following ways :-

(1) by payment of Mahr to the wife;

(2) if the wife is major, after marriage at any time she can relinquish the Mahr or part of her Mahr in favour of her husband of his heirs and this type of relinquishment would be valid even without consideration or the consent of the heirs; or

(3) by transfer of property to the wife in lieu of Mahr ; or

(4) by satisfaction from the usufruct of the husband's property in exercise of the widow's lien according to

(5) by recovery through the Court-

(a) from the husband or his heirs, or

(b) subject to the provisions from a person including the guardian himself who has stood as a surety for dower, or

(c) from the father if he made the contract of marriage for his minor son who died without leaving any property, or

(d) by mutual agreement or by some family arrangement.

1. Payment of Mahr

Where payment were made from time to time in varying amounts and there is no evidence that husband allocated any of these payments to the dower debt, nor was there any attempt at the trail to show that the lady accepted them as such, it cannot be said that the Mahr debt was satisfied by such payments. On the other hand, the provision is not correct that payments of money by Shia husband to his wife during the continuance of their married life should be presumed to be payments of her Mahr debt and that it should be for her to establish the contrary.

But this depends upon the facts of each case and it may be presumed from the circumstances that the payment was made towards dower. Lapse of time since marriage and the fact that the husband has been in a position to pay the dower raises no presumption that the Mahr had been actually paid. The burden lies on the person alleging that the Mahr had been paid to prove it. A payment to the guardian of a minor of insane wife or to the father or grandfather of a virgin would give an effective discharge. Some payment may be made for satisfaction of Mahr by mutual agreement or some sort family arrangement may be made or life-interest transferred.

2. Oral Gift in lieu of Wife's Mahr is Valid

The oral gift made by a Muslim in favour of his wife in lieu of her Mahar debt is valid Under Section 129 of the Transfer of Property Act saves Muslim gifts from the application of the provisions of Chapter- VII of the Transfer of Property Act.

3. Surety of Mahlr

The contract of surety-ship for Mahr has been expressly provided for Muslim Law. A father may make a contract for Mahr on behalf of a minor son (whether before or after or at the marriage) and the contract would be binding on the son if it is made during minority. Here it is not correct to say that a father by giving his consent to the marriage automatically becomes a surety for the payment of the dower debt. If, however the father has contracted the marriage of a minor son, who dies without leaving any property he is liable to the wife for dower. But it is valid for a person who is a guardian (whether for husband or the wife or for both) to stand a surety for payment of dower although the wife may be minor. Where a father contracts the marriage of his daughter (whether a child, an adult, a virgin or insane) and stands as a surety the surety ship is valid and she has the option of suing the husband or the guardian. If he has become a surety by the direction of the husband, he may have recourse against the husband. When a father contracts the marriage of his infant son and stands as a surety, the surety-ship would be valid if the woman or some on else on her behalf accepts it. In this case, the wife can claim the dower from the guardian but she is not entitled to demand if from the husband till he attains puberty. The father has no right of reimbursement from the son unless there was a condition in the original security that he should be entitled to such reimbursement and as to a guardian standing surety while suffering from death-illness. A stranger may also make a contract of surety-ship for dower.

In Shia's school of law when the marriage of an infant son is contracted by his father and the child is poor, the obligation rest entirely on the father and in the event of his death must be discharged out of the whole of his property, whether the child should arrive at maturity and become wealthy or die before it.

4. Transfer of Property in lieu of Mahr

A husband may validly make a transfer of his property to his wife in lieu of Mahr even the Mahr has not fallen due. Section 53 of Transfer of Property Act says that when a transfer is made with a view to defeat or delay creditors the creditors can avoid it Under Section 53. It was held in Bibi Kabra Vs. Jainandan Prasad[22] that the section applies to the Muslim also and covers all communities.

There is no rule of Muslim Law which may be inconsistent with the provisions of this section. But Muslim Law also made its analogous provisions against fraudulent transfer. A gift made by a person in insolvent circumstances may be set aside at the instance of the creditors, if the gift was intended to defraud them. It is well known that Muslim marriage is as same contractual dowers features to some extent and seems to be for marriage is the consideration and that a *transfer in lieu of dower is in nature of a Hiba-bil-Ewaz.* In that context, the Kabinama was the document of transfer and contained in it the relevant agreement or contract of transfer in writing. It was held that of course Kabinama is not registered, but even if it required registration, having regard to the fact that defendant No. 1 was put in possession of the disputed property in pursuance of that contract and the further fact that defendant No.1 has married the plaintiffs son Ayub in terms of or in accordance with her said contract and thus performed her part of the same. Section 53-A of the Transfer of Property Act would preclude the plaintiff from enforcing any rights against defendant No.1 in respect of the disputed property inconsistent with or not mentioned in the said contract. The said Section 53-A of the Transfer of Property Act would, accordingly, bar the plaintiffs of present suit.

The question whether the transaction is really transfer of property or sham or simulated transaction must be decided on the particular facts of a case. If dower is really not due and a fictitious transfer is made through collusive arbitration proceedings, it can be avoided. In Mohammad Ali Mohammad Khan Vs. Mst. Bismillah Begam[23] the defendant 2, from 1913 was carrying on a business which to a certain extent was of a hazardous character and he had the opportunity of utilizing the money of the appellant for his own purposes and the effect of the deed of gift certainly would be the defeat or delay and claim which the appellant might have at any time against him. Their lordships are of opinion that defendant 2 was always the true owner and in possession of the property which was the subject matter of the gift from the time of his purchase in 1913 and 1915 respectively and that this deed was false and fraudulent. Such transfers can be avoided to the extent to which they are fictitious. But a debtor can prefer some of his creditors to others. The burden of proving that the transaction was fraudulent or colorable lies on the party challenging the transfer. The widow being a creditor for her dower debt a transfer in lieu of dower will be valid if the dower is really due even if other creditors are defeated. Such a transaction cannot be impeached Under Section 53 of the Transfer of Property Act, 1882. Such alienation is not fraudulent. It is well established law that a Mohammedan widow has a right to payment of her dower debt. The right does not amount to a charge on the property but if the widow is in possession at the death of her husband she is allowed to retain possession until the debt is paid. If a widow wishes to forestall other creditors and to obtain what is due to her first, there is nothing fraudulent in her action in carrying such wish. The transfer to the wife requires her acceptance. Such a transfer cannot be challenged on any of the following grounds :-

(1) That it was made in lieu of deferred dower which had not become due. The husband may payoff the dower debt even if it has not become due. The question, whether the dower was to be prompt or deferred is of minor importance as satisfaction of deferred dower debt can be valid consideration for a transfer between the husband and the wife.

(2) That the debt has become time barred. A transfer in lieu of a time barred debt is valid.

(3) That a deduction might have been made by the Court, if a suit for dower had been filed in the Court.

(4) That the transfer was made while a suit by a creditor against the husband was pending.

(5) That the marriage was void. The consideration would in such case be only void and no unlawful.

(6) That a transfer of the property was made only to a limited extent, or was conditional or contingent. If it is not so limited, the wife would become absolute owner and a sale by her cannot be challenged.

(7) That the transfer has been made after the dower had already been paid off. The: deed should be construed as one of advancement. The deed is also valid because it is open to the husband to increase the dower at any time. Such transfer can be challenged only on proof of circumstances indicated in Section 53 of the Transfer of Property Act, 1882.

(8) That the husband was not the owner of the property when he made the transfer, acquiring title to it afterwards. In such case, a court of equity will compel the husband to perform the contract. The entire property would pass to her under the principle of feeding the estoppels.

Wife's Right of Retention of the Property in lieu of Mahr

As in earlier pages has been to explain that the right of Mahr is similar to the right of an unsecured creditor. Here Muslim Law gives and confers a special advantage on the woman keeping in view their *financial needs and weak socio economic conditions in which they* find themselves. This privilege is known as the right of the retaining the property of the husband which law fully came to be in possession of the widow or divorcee.

The right of retention means that the Muslim Woman whose marriage has been dissolved by death or divorce has a right to continue to hold the possession of her husbands' property till her dowel-debt is justified this right of retention of the possession of her husbands' estate is not available to a wife during the subsistence of the marriage unless the proves a contact under which acquired a right of lien or possession over her husbands' property. The divorcees as well as widow have a legal right to receive the dower amount from the property of the husband if the same remains unpaid at the time of death of deceased or the date on which marriage tie stands finally dissolved. It is clear from the earlier pages of this thesis. The right of the wife to retain property arises provided the following conditions are satisfied that is first she must have entered into possession of the property lawfully and without force and fraud and secondly there must be debt due to her in respect of her dower and she should make a claim in respect of that dower. If these conditions are satisfied, then the wife is entitled to retain possession of the property till the debt is discharged. This privilege has its origin in the personal law of Indian Muslims. The principle derives its legitimacy from demands of public welfare which to be meaningful must confer some added legal advantages on those who unfortunately are obliged to face problems mostly beyond their reach. It is a special right by of a Muslim widow/

divorcee recognized by Muslim Law that she has right to the possession of the property of her deceased husband in lieu of dower debt. Muslim widow / divorcee right to the possession of her deceased husband in lieu of dower debt.

The nature of the right seems to be referable to the rule of the pure Muslim Law that any creditor of a deceased Muslim is entitled to the help himself to any money or chattels to repay him out of the proceeds. This general rule of Muslim Law is fully applicable in the present age. The widow / divorcee's right to retain the possession in lieu of her dower debt has sprung from this not from the contract. The basic normative principle is that the possession must have been obtained lawfully end not by employment of any dubious stratagem because this rule represents more equity than law. So where fraud or force or deception has been employed, the right to retain the estate of the husband till the satisfaction of the dower-claim shall be lost. Accordingly to Muslim Law a widow as well divorcee is entitled to remain in possession of the property of her husband if she gets possession of the property lawfully and with force and fraud even though the dower has not been ascertained or has been left to be subsequently settled and she is entitled to retain that possession until her dower is satisfied. The heirs or the creditors or alive can not disturb her possession unless they satisfy the dower debt. She is entitled to retain possession till it is satisfied from the usufruct. A divorcee/ widow right to retain possession of her husbands' estate in lieu of her dower is for a special purpose. It is by way of compulsion to obtain speedy payment of the dower, which is an unsecured debt.

The tentative right is the debt and the share. The adjective right is retention. Though she has no greater right than that of any other unsecured creditor, yet if she obtains possession of the deceased husbands' property lawfully and without force or fraud, she is entitled to held it until her debt is satisfied. The Calcutta High Court in the decision of Asia Khatun Vs. Amarendra Nath Basu[24] held that" the right to retention of the husband's property arises for the first time on the termination of the marriage either by the death of the husband or by divorce but there is no such right during the continuance of the marriage." The Peshawar High Court in Ch. Shakar S.Dass Vs. Mahbub Jan[25] through Alnsond J.C. and Mr. Justice Mir Ahmed observed that "A Mohammedan widow who claims to have entered into possession of her husbands' property on claim of her dower is entitled to remain in possession until her dower is satisfied."

As earlier mentioned in the previous lines that a widow / divorcee's right to retain possession of her husband's estate in lieu of her dower is for special purpose. It is by way of compulsion to obtain speedy payment of the dower which is an unsecured debt. Where she is not in possession or has lost possession, she cannot claim to obtain it. Because her right to retain is not in the nature of a charge on the property like in mortgage but a personal right against the heirs and creditors of her deceased / former husband. The leading case on the point is Babee Bachun Vs. Hamid Hussain[26] where it was held that the possession of the husbands' estate should have been acquired by the wife without force or fraud, that is it should be peacefully and lawfully acquired. A Division Bench of Patna High Court in Abdul

Rehman Vs. Wali Mohammad[27] held through Chief Justice Dawron Miller and Mr. Justice Mullick that according to Muslim Law the widow has the right to possess the property of her husband in lieu of the dower debt, and so long as her dower debt remains unsatisfied and she does not transfer the dower debt itself, she can transfer for her life time possession of the property.

The judicial scenario of the privileged right of retention can be made through the studies of cases.

In the similar decision of Mst. Bibi Makbul Unnisa Vs. Mst. Bibi Urnat-un-Nisa;[28] Mr. Justice Courtte and Mr. Justice Das held that the right of widow to hold the property as a security for the dower debt and to continue in possession there of until the dower debt was satisfied, was both heritable and transferable. The authority of both these decisions; Abdur Rehman Vs. Wali Mohammad & Mst.Bibi Ummatmiya[29] have been shaken by a subsequent decision of the Privy Council in Mst. Maina Bibi Vs. Vakil Ahmed[30] in which widow of the deceased Muslim was in possession of her husband's estate in lieu of her unpaid dower and the heirs of deceased obtained a decree against her to the effect that they should have possession of their share of the estate upon payment of a proportionate part of the dower debt within six months and that upon failure to pay there suit should be dismissed In Maina Bibi Vs. Chaudhary Vakil Ahmed Supreme Court has held that a Muslim widow in possession of her husbands' estate in lieu of her claims for dower remaining unpaid whether with the consent of the heirs or otherwise is not entitled to priority as against his other unsecured creditors. In this case a Muslim named Muin-ud-din died in

1890 possessed of immovable property, the subject of the present litigation. He was survived by his widow, the appellant Maina Bibi, who entered into possession of his property. In 1902, the plaintiff, respondents in the present suit, sued the widow, claiming immediate possession of their shares of estate. The widow pleaded that the estate was a gift to her by her husband, and alternatively that she was entitled to possession until her dower was paid. The Trial Judges in 1903 made a decree for possession on condition that the plaintiffs paid to widow Rs.25,387 within six months, and the decree provided that in default of payment the suit should be dismissed. An appeal to the High Court was dismissed, the time for the payment being extended to December, 1906. The plaintiffs respondents did not pay the money and the widow remained in possession. In 1907, Maina Bibi executed two deeds of gift to her husband's estate in favour of the defendant's appellants, to whom she gave possession. The terms of the deeds appear from the judgment; by them the widow purported to convey an absolute title. The plaintiff respondents filed the present suit in 1915 against the widow, Maina Bibi and her alienate, the defendants-appellants. The plaintiff claimed that the widow could not according to Muslim Law transfer the properties. They claimed possession unconditionally or alternatively upon payment of the proportionate amount of the dower debt, after deducing the profits of the property. The defendants pleaded among other things that the decree of 1902 affirmed in 1906, operated as Res-Judicate ; further that the claim was barred by limitation. It has been held that the right to hold possession cannot be served from the dower debt and transferred as a separate interest. In the course of the Judgment of Lord Atkinson has stated that "It was contended as their Lordships understood that Mst. Maina Bibi had by the deeds of 1907 assigned both her dower debt and her right to hold possession of her husband's estate until that debt was paid. It is doubtful whether she could have done either of these things, but however, that may be, it is clear, she in fact never purported or attempted to do either of them. On the contrary, in those deeds she describes herself as the absolute owner of the property of her deceased husband, and purports to convey that absolute ownership of her donee. " Further their Lordships observed that "There is no ground for the contention, if it has been really put forward, that because these deeds fail to effect a transfer of the absolute interest with which they purport to deal, they operate to transfer the widow's dower debt and her right to hold possession of the lands till that debt is paid. By giving up the possession of the lands, as in her deeds she alleges she has done, she has undoubtedly lost her right to hold the possession of them."

The decision of the Judicial committee in Mst.Maina Bibi Vs. Vakil Ahmed overrides by implication the previous decisions of this High Court in Abdul Rahman Vs. Wali Mohammad[31] and Mst.Bibi Makbulnissa Vs.Mst.Bibi Umat-un-Nisa[32] and the view expressed in these two Patna decision is therefore no longer authorities. In Shaikh Mohammad Zubair Vs. Mst. Bibi Sahidan[33] it was observed by Mr. Justice Shearer that" the dower debt of Muslim widow is not, properly speaking a charge upon the property in her husband, and the interest which she has in the property in her possession in lieu of dower debt is therefore an interest restricted in its enjoyment to her personally within the meaning of Section 6 (d) of Transfer of Property Act and as such is not capable of alienation. In a later case, of Ramprasad Vs. Bibi Khodaijatul[34] a Division Bench consisting of Mr.1ustice Manohar Lal expressed this view that a widow who was in possession of her husband's property in lieu of her dower debt could not mortgage her right of possession. It was held by both the Learned Judges in the case that the previous decision of the Patna High Court in Abdul Rehman V s. Wali Mohammad was no longer a good law in view of the decision of the Privy Council in Mst. Maina Bibi Vs. Vakil Ahmed.

This right of retention comes into existence for the first time on the dissolution of the marriage either by the death of the husband or by divorce and she is entitled to retain until her dower debt is satisfied. The Possession of the property of the husband by the widow may be presumed to be on the ground of its being a lien for dower, where possession is obtained and continued after the death of the husband, there is a presumption that it was legally and peacefully obtained. It is for the heirs to prove that the possession is not in lieu of dower as it was held in Mohd. Karimullah Vs.Amam Begum.[35] In Cooverbai Nasarwanji Bulsara Vs. Hayatbi Budhan Bai[36] where Rahim-un-Nisa's possession was not that of a co-tenant for the possession of a co-widow in Muslim Law in lieu of her dower, does not represent the possession of the other widow of her heirs. The possession in assumed in her own personal and independent right. The presumption which the Muslim Law has designed for the benefit of the widow, as a means of protection to her right having been specially safeguarded in the Quran is a presumption of law but a presumption of fact, depending upon the circumstances of each particular case. If she has a lien over the property then she would have such lien till her dower debt is discharged. This is well established and would be clear from decision of the Privy Council in Mst. Bebee Bachun Vs. Hamid Hussain[37]. It would be useful to quote the observation of their Lordships of the Privy Council in this context. Their Lordship's observations are as follows - "Whatever right may be called, it appears, to be founded on the power of the widow as a creditor for her dower to hold the property of her husband of which she has lawfully and without force or fraud obtained possession until her debt is satisfied. The Allahabad High Court through Mr. Justice Mohd. Akbar in Asia Khatun Vs. Amarendra Nath Babu[38] held that "The right to retention of the husband's property arises for the first time on the demission of the marriage either by the death of the husband or by divorce but there is no such right during the continuance of the marriage." The Peshawar High Court in Ch.Shankar Dass Vs. Mahbub Jan[39] through Almond J.C. and Mr. Justice Mir Ahmed observed that "A Muslim widow who claims to have entered into possession of her husband's property on claim of her dower is entitled to remain in possession until her dower is satisfied."

A Muslim husband may settle any amount that he likes by way of dower debt upon his wife though it may be beyond his means and though nothing may be left to his heirs after the payment of the amount but he cannot in any case settle less than ten Dirhams. In Mirvahedali Kadumiya Vs. Rashidbeg Kadumiya,[40] It has been held that where a Mohammedan widow, who is in possession of her husband's property still claims the dower debt due to her then her right to retain possession of the property till the dower debt is discharged exists and it is immaterial in what character whether as a creditor for dower debt or otherwise she came into possession of the property, provided she came into possession lawfully and without force or fraud. Such right to retain possession can also be exercised by her heirs after her death. The widow has no legal right to get into possession of the property. She is only entitled to retain possession if she gets into it. There is no right to recover possession except under Section 9 of the Societies Registration Act. But if she lawfully and peacefully gets into possession without any agreement she would be entitled to retain it. Whether it is necessary that before the widow becomes entitled for the retention of the property, she must obtain the consent of the heirs? It is a controversial question to answer. There is a conflict of opinions among the Indian High Courts on this question.

In the matter the Privy Council observed in Hamira Bibi Vs. Zubaida Bibi[41] at that "her right however is no greater than that of any other unsecured creditor, except that if she lawfully, with the express or implied consent of the husband or his other heirs, obtains possession of the whole or part of his estate, to satisfy her claim with the rents and issues accruing, therefore, she is entitled to retain such possession until it is satisfied." The controversy arises due to different views taken by different High Courts of the above quoted exposition of law by the Privy Council.

The Allahabad High Court held, dissenting from earlier cases to the contrary, that the observations of the Privy Council in the above case were obiter dicta and did not make it necessary as precedent that widow's possession should have been obtained by the consent of the heirs. In other words, she is entitled to retain possession if she gets into it lawfully and without force or fraud, even though without the consent of the heirs.

The Bombay, Oudh, Lahore, Peshawr and the Madras High Courts also agree with this view. It has also been held that it was necessary that the widow should have taken possession upon a claim for her dower; that the character of her possession must be that of creditor and no other character. Further, contrary to it, the Calcutta[42] and Patna[43] High Courts are of opinion that the observations of Privy Council were not merely obiter dicta and the widow is entitled to retain possession only if she gets into possession with the consent of the heirs. It has also been held again in a later Allahabad case of Shaikh Mohd. Zubair Vs. Bibi Suhidan[44] that the consent of the heirs is necessary. but in Abdul Wahab Vs. Mushtaque Ahmed[45] mutation was effected in favour of Rasul Bandi after the death of Atullah. Abdul Syed made no objection whatsoever and that is enough under the Muslim Law to show that Rasul Bandi entered into possession lawfully in lieu of her dower, without any force or fraud. It may be pointed out that the later view is not sound. In another Privy Council decision it was held that the widow was entitled to a lien if she got into possession "lawfully and without force or fraud". There is no reference to the question of the consent of heirs. A later Privy

Council's case of Mst.Maina Bibi Vs. Vakil Ahmad[46] while dealing with the subject, does not make any suggestion as the necessity of the consent of the heirs for the right being available to the widow, explaining the reasons, In Aziz-un-Nisa's case,[47] it was observed that "All that is necessary for the widow to retain possession until her dower debt is paid is that she should obtain possession not by force or fraud. She is in the position of a creditor and having obtained possession lawfully she is entitled to hold possession until her dower debt is satisfied. The consent of the heirs is not essential. She has to depend upon consent of heirs that consent she will seldom get and the rule will become nugatory." Tayabji[48], the noted Scholar of Islamic Law has opined that the widow's possession is legally required to be 'peaceful and lawful' and in such situation consent of either husband or in case of his death other legitimate heirs' is an implied feature of such possession. In view of another Learned Scholar Fyzee[49], the requirement of the consent is meaningless in view of the true nature of the widow's right of retention in lieu of her dower-debt. There is a legal presumption of lawfulness (of the acquisition of possession) in favour of a widow who has been in possession in her husband's life time and continuous to do so after his death. It has been reiterated by the High Court of Bombay that in such case it is not necessary to prove the prior consent of the heirs on the part of the widow who had taken possession on account of unpaid dower.

The analysis of judicial pronouncements reveals that the question of necessity of consent on this controversial issue, the discussed pronouncements stress that the consent of the heirs is not essential, appears to be correct and same is in consonance with the spirit of law providing a special protection to a Muslim woman for realization of dower-debt. If she is dependent of consent to get the retention, the basic object of the special right i.e. 'widow's right of retention' shall be meaningless and the weaker section of the society cannot avail the special right and she shall not be in position by virtue of this right to enforce and get the payment of dower-debt.

Right to Retention & Alienation

The special right of retention simply arms the widow only to retain the possession and appropriate the usufruct of the property till the satisfaction of dower-debt. This right does not give her any proprietary right in the property of her deceased husband. It follows that she has no right to alienate the property by sale. mortgage, gift or otherwise. Fate of alienation may be discussed in the light of judicial pronouncements. In Mst. Fahiman Vs. Bulaq[50] Mr. Justice Nanarutty and Mr. Justice Zia-ul-Hassan referred to with approval the observation of The Chief Justice Stuart and Mr. Justice Raza in Sitaram Bibi Vs. Ganesh Prasad[51] and held that "the right of the widow to retain possession of her husband's property until satisfaction of the dower debt does not carry with it the right of selling, mortgaging or otherwise transferring the property and that if she alienates the property itself and delivers the possession thereof to the alienee, her husband's other heirs are entitled to recover possession of the property from the alienee without payment to him of the dower debt." The Patna High Court in the case of Mst. Bibi Makbulunnisa

Vs. Mst. Umat-un-Nisa,[52] Mr. Justice Cutts and Mr.Justice Das observed that" The position is different where there is sale of the property and not an assignment of the security. This distinction has not always been kept in view in the numerous cases which have been decided on the point, but the distinction is an important one and cannot be ignored. The right to hold property as security for the dower debt and to continue in possession thereof until the dower debt is satisfied is property, and both heritable and transferable. The Court further held that "but the widow has no proprietary title in the property, except to the extent of her share therein, and where she purports to sell the property, and not security only, the sale is utterly ineffectual so as to confer any title on the vendee" Allahabad High Court held that a Muslim widow in possession of immovable property of her late husband in lieu of her dower, has no power to mortgage such property. If the widow alienates the retained property, the alienation is valid to the extent of her own share and it does not affect the shares of the other heirs of her husband. In earlier case of Chuni Bibi Vs. Shams-un-Nissa Bibi[53], it has been held that the widow who is in possession of her husband's estate in lieu of dower is not competent to alienate the whole estate permanently but can only sell what belonged to her by right of inheritance.

In Ajuba Begum Vs. Nazir Ahmed[54] a widow claimed to be in possession of the moiety in lieu of dower and she purported jointly with the owner of other moiety of the house to sell the whole of it to a third person. It was held that she could only have transferred to the third person the rights which she acquired by inheritance in her husband's property and could not have passed her entire right, even if she had been validly in possession of the moiety of the house in lieu of dower and the deed passed nothing more to the vendee than the widow's inherited right in house. The same view was adopted in another case of Shaikh Salima Vs. Shaikh Mohd. In the case of Abdul Kadar[55] it was observed that only the widow's share in the property passed to the transferee.

But the early pronouncement of Allahabad High Court[56] held that where the widow sells or gifts the property, the transfer is void altogether so as not to take effect to the extent even of the widow's share. The Chief Justice Edge and Mr. Justice Banerji in this case observed that "It has been held on several occasions in this court that a Muslim widow in possession in lieu of her dower cannot sell any portion of the property. She cannot give a good title to any portion of the property, in as much as her position is only that of a widow in possession in lieu of her dower." So the mortgage granted by the widow was held to be inoperative and it passed no title to the property. Mulla doubts in respect of the correctness of the view because there is no justification in this view. On the basis of majority decision it is submitted that if the widow sells or makes gift of the property, the sale of gift is valid to the extent of her own share in the property. This judicial approach sets the position on right direction and on pious foundation based on the Islam.

These majority decisions remove the confusion created by some above discussed judicial pronouncements and re-establishes the absolute, ownership of the widow by virtue of inheritance and to the extent of her own share in the property, she has absolute right to transfer.

Heritability and the Right of Retention

Under the Islamic Property Law, the dower constitutes the property right of woman so this right to property is capable of descending to the heirs of the widow on her death provided, it is unpaid. The unpaid dower becomes due and realizable and can be recovered not only the widow herself but also by her heirs. When the widow dies her dower devolves on her heirs because dower is a debt like all other debts. The diversity of judicial opinion as to whether the right to retain possession of the property by a widow in lieu of dower debt is heritable under scrutiny and researcher's quest for truth is to be satisfied regarding the contribution of Indian Judiciary. The judicial views are examined in two categories right is heritable and right is not heritable in following pages.

When a widow who has held possession of her deceased husband's property in lieu of her dower, dies without having recovered the dower, her heirs according to one set of judicial decisions succeed to her right of possession. The judicial view of High Courts are as follows: Mr. Justice Abdur Rahim in Beeju Bee Vs. Syed Murtuza[57] speaking through the Madras High Court observed that" On principle the rights of the widow to retain possession till the satisfaction of her dower debt, must in my opinion be held as against the claim of the heirs to be a right capable of descending to her heirs. "The court has supported the view on the basis of sound reasoning. The law gives her right not because she is the widow of her deceased husband but in her capacity as one of his creditors. When the widow dies, all her rights of this nature of or in connection with the property devolve under the Muslim Law to her heirs and there seems to be no reason to make an exception to the rule with respect to this right of heirs, which would often be a very valuable right. Thus, according to the Madras High Court the right to hold possession till the satisfaction of the dower debt is heritable. The Bombay High Court[58] has held that the right to hold possession is heritable. In an illustrative case of Chunni Bibi Vs. Shans-un-nissa Bibi[59] Scott C.J., and Mr. Justice Shah observed that "It is substantial right and under circumstances it would be practically a right in substitution of the claim for dower, where the amount of dower is large and far in excess of the value of the property of which the widow has obtained possession and where there is no property of the husband as in the present case, the right of the widow to hold the property in lieu of her dower is the only right left and in our opinion it is substantial right as her claim to dower and it should, therefore, be capable of descending to her heirs." In a later case.[60] the question before this court was whether the heirs were entitled to retain certain properties till the dower due to the widow had been paid and whether this claim was justified according to Muslim Law. Mr. Justice Chagla (as he was then) observed that "It is clearly established that the debt in respect of dower is enforceable not only by the wife but also by her heirs. It is further established that the right of possession is a heritable right and not only the wife is entitled to retain possession but also her heirs. As soon as she or her heirs put forward the claim for dower, the possession becomes the possession of the creditor of the estate and the creditor has the right to retain the property till that debt was discharged." Thus, according to the Bombay High Court, the right to retain the property till the satisfaction of dower-debt is heritable. The Patna High Court[61] in series of its pronouncements as a security for the dower-debt and to continue in possession thereof until the debts is satisfied, is property and, therefore, heritable. The court in recent pronouncement:

Mst.Haliman Vs. Mohd. Monir[62] reiterated the well settled law concerning the widow's right in respect of her dower debt and its heritability, relying on the Bombay High Court in Mirvahidali Vs. Rashid Beg[63] the court held that where a Muslim widow came into possession of her husband's property, lawfully and without force or fraud and still claimed dower debt, her right to retain the property existed and it could be exercised by her heirs as well after her death. The Allahabad High Court in Abdul Wahab Khan Vs. Mustaq Ahmed Khan[64] held that though the widow may not be in actual possession of this right, yet her heirs would succeed to this right as well besides her other properties, if any. Thus her right of retention is admittedly a heritable right. This court in majority of cases has held that the right to retain property is always a right to property and is, therefore, capable of devolving to her heirs on her death. In the case of Ali Baksh Vs. Allahdbad Khan[65] Mr. Justice Tudball seems to have inclined to look upon such a right as property which under the ordinary law would be heritable. The sole question for determination in this case was whether the heirs of a Muslim widow who has lawfully attained possession of her husband's estate in lieu of her dower, are entitled to continue in possession of that estate after her death, until the dower-debt has been discharged. Mr. Justice Tudball observed that "Such a right is property and prime facie, in the absence of any law to the contrary, it is property which is heritable. It is very easy to conceive a case in which a widow has held such possession of many years over and above the period of limitation, within which she must sue for her dower-debt and has then died without debt being fully discharged. If the heirs are not entitled to inherit, they lose all means of recovering the balance of debt due of course, if the widow agrees with her husband's other heirs to hold the property only for her life-time in full satisfaction of the debt, the latter is extinguished on her death. In the absence of any such contract, the widow's heirs are entitled to inherit the right to continue in possession until her dower-debt is satisfied." The Court relied on Azizullah Khan Vs. Ahmed Ali Khan[66] where it was held by the Bench of the same court (Oldfeild and Mahmood, JJ) that the heirs of the widow in possession in lieu of dower succeeded to her estate including the dower-debt and as such were entitled to continue in possession of the deceased husband's property like the widow until the dower-debt is satisfied. This case was parallel to the one before Justice Mr. Tudball and was a ruling in point. It was an express ruling to the effect that the widow's right to retain possession is heritable. In a latter case of Abdullah Vs. Sharns-ul-Haq[67] the heritability of the right of retention has been conceded, but the widow's heirs have been held not entitled to usurp possession of her husband's property for her unpaid dower if widow heirs has not been in possession. The Learned Judge in this case observed that "If the widow has peacefully got the possession of her husband's estate after his death the right which she had to remain in possession may descend to her heirs, but where the widow never got into possession her heirs are not entitled to remain in possession for her unsatisfied dower debt." This view of the Court was later on followed in another case of Ameer Hasan Vs. Md. Nazar Hasan[68] where the Learned Judge observed that" The widow may have a right to retain possession but has no legal right to go into possession, her right is that if she gets peaceably into possession without force or fraud, she is entitled to remain in possession until her dower debt is paid. If the widow has no legal right to take possession, such a right i.e. to go into possession cannot descend to her heirs because she never had it". Dealing with the nature of heritability Mr. Justice Niamatullah also observed that: "The: right of a Mohammadan widow, who has entered into possession of her husband's property peacefully and without force or fraud in lieu of her dower debt, has been held by this court to be heritable so as to entitle her heirs to remain in possession until the debt is satisfied. The possession of heirs who inherited not only her right to receive the dower but also her right to remain in possession, is, thus, not upon to question." The perusal of foregoing judicial pronouncements reveals that the right and claim of widow of unpaid dower against the property of the deceased husband is heritable and the heirs of the widow can inherit provided the possession of widow is lawfully without force and fraud is established. Under Muslim Law dower constitutes the exclusive and absolute property of woman and it is established under the Islamic concept of property that is subject to rule of inheritance and by operation of law same is subject to division among legal and legitimate heirs. So, in view of this fact, the approach of judiciary in interpreting and applying to the facts and situations is quite justified and Islamic in notion and outlook.

The widow's right to retention of her deceased husbands' property in lieu of dower is purely a personal right and is, therefore, incapable of surviving to the heirs of widow after her death. Leading case on the point is Hadi Ali V s. Akbar Ali.[69] The relevant facts of the case are that Akbar Ali brought a suit against Huran Bibi, the widow of Karim Baksh and Hadi Ali, the donee of a portion of the property from Huran Bibi, to recover possession of his share out of the estate of his deceased uncle Karim Baksh. Hadi Ali is the son of a daughter of Karim Baksh, who predeceased him. The court of first instance decreed the claim and an appeal was preferred by the widow and Hadi Ali's appeal had preference to that portion of that estate which was not included in the gift to Hadi Ali and during the pendency of the appeal Huran died. The court held that the appeal of Huran abated on the ground that as Hadi Ali was not brought upon the record in the place of Huran and as her three daughter's who were living did not apply to be made parties to the appeal within the time allowed by the law and so far as the property in respect of which the appeal is concerned, the decree of court of First Instance became final. As regards property which is subject of alleged gift to Hadi Ali, the lower Appellate Court has found that Huran was in possession of it in lieu of dower. Having been put into possession in lieu of her dower, she was entitled to continue in possession so long as her dower debt remained unpaid; that was a right of personal nature to her and became extinct on her death. Hadi Ali is not entitled to remain in possession of the estate left by Karim Baksh. The result is that Akbar Ali is entitled to the decree granted to him by the Court of first instance, from this Judgment, Hadi Ali appealed; Edge C.J. and Mr. Justice Burkit observed that "The Lower Appellate Court has decided that a lien for her dower which a Muslim widow had obtained on lands of her husband was purely personal right and did not survive to her heirs. This decision is supported by Ali Mohammad Khan V s. Azizullah Khan.[70]

It is submitted that the case was similar in its aspects to that of Ali Mohd. Khan Vs. Azizullah Khan and also Ajuba Begum Vs. Nazir Ahmed and in the latter case Mr. Justice Mahmood pointed out the these decisions were not inconsistent with his decision in Azizullah Khan Vs. Ahmed Ali Khan wherein he held that the widow's right to retain possession lawfully obtained was heritable. Mr.Justice Mahmood made a clear distinction between the circumstances in the present case that "The position of heirs who upon the death of a Muslim widow, who was in possession in lieu of dower, succeed to her estate including her claim to dower, is vastly distinguishable from the position of a purchaser from her, of an isolated piece of immovable property such as the house in this case. Such a purchaser is in one sense the representative of the widow but he is not her legal heirs would be. He is not her representative in the sense in which upon her death her heirs would be. He is not her representative for her claim to dower, because it is a money claim by itself and stands upon a specific property." It is respectfully submitted that the reasoning of the Learned Judge that the widow's right to continue in possession is a right personal to her and extinct on her death and not surviving to her heirs is not acceptable. Further submitted that the judgment is very brief and same is not supported by any authoritatively text of Muslim Law or any rule of law, i.e. either English or Indian for its justification. No reason is given to hold that the widow's right to continue in possession extinct on her death. Though, the reliance is placed on Mr.Justice Mohmood's pronouncement in Ajuba Begum Vs. Nazir Ahmed,[71] but it may be pointed out that no mention is made of his ruling in Azizullah Khan Vs. Ahmed Ali Mohammad nor clear distinction which he draws in his judgment between the circumstances of the case before him and those of the Azizullah Khan Vs. Ajmed Ali Moharnmad.[72] Keeping in view the difference to Mr.Jusitcie Mahmood it does not seem that he held that the widow had a lien which did not survive to her heirs. Virtually it is difficult to understand why the right which is an incident of the claim to dower and is capable of being enjoyed as a mere personal right, when the principal right of which it is an incident is not so treated according to Muslim Law. It may be that after the widow has had possession for several years, her claim to dower may be time barred, and she would care only for the right to hold the property in lieu of dower. The heirs would not care to have any accounts taken when it is clear that proceeds fall for short of amount due to the widow. The right to possession of property appears to be quite a substantive right and there seems to be no reason to treat it as a personal one when the claim to dower is a heritable right, for instance, if a widow does not obtain possession of her husband's property and sues against heirs in respect of her dower, she can obtain a decree and bring the property to sell. She would obtain the proceeds of the sale and these proceeds would devolve on her heirs. There is no reason why the alternative right, which a Muslim widow has of holding the property of her husband, with the liability to account, in lieu of her dower, should not devolve on her heirs on her death. Thus the analysis of leading pronouncements having the bearing and direct relevant to the subject under study for purpose of research, reveals that in view of Bombay,[73] Madras,[74] Patna,[75] Mysore,[76] Nagpur,[77] and Oudh High Courts this right is definitely heritable. The Allahabad High Court in its earlier decision of Hadi Ali Vs. Akbar Ali took the view against its heritability, but the authority of later cases decided by the Allahabad High Court is distinctly against the earlier view and now this Court is of the view that this right is heritable. Thus the judicial view in majority of cases support that the right is heritable and the heirs are entitled to claim it even if the dower amount has not been demanded by the wife in her life time. Now the conflict is resolved by the Supreme Court of India holding that the right to hold possession in lieu of dower-debt is heritable through the decision of Kapoor Chand Vs. Kidar Nissa.[78]

Transferability and the Right of Retention

The Judiciary has divergent view as to whether the right to retain possession of her deceased husband's property by widow in lieu of dower is transferable. One: set of opinion is that the right to retain possession is a right to property and is, therefore, transferable on the same analogy its heritability is favoured by judiciary. The other set of opinion is quite contrary to this, the lien which the widow has over the estate of her husband, is purely a personal right, and it cannot, therefore, be transferred. It is undisputed that a Muslim widow has the right to assign dower-debt. But it is unsettled whether her right to hold and retain possession of her husband's estate till dower is paid, is transferable and only for the period of her life, and whether if transferable, it may be transferred only with the right to dower, or whether the right to hold possession may be transferred by itself without assignment of the right to the payment of the: dower. The right of lieu does not confer any titled to the property in the wife. The title remains in the heirs including the wife. She is entitled only to a lien. The right of the widow to retain possession of her husband's property until satisfaction of the dower-debt does not carry with it the right of selling, mortgaging or gifting or otherwise transferring the property. If he transfers the property, the transfer is utterly ineffectual except to the extent of the interest of the widow herself.

Judicial Analysis of this Complicated Issue

The various High Courts hold the view that the right to hold the property as a security for the dower-debt and to continue in possession thereof until the debt is satisfied constitutes property right and therefore it is transferable. In Beeju Bee Vs. Syed Moorthuja[79] Mr. Justice Abdur Rahim after a detailed examination of the law on the point observed that " there is no express text of Mohammedan Law so far as one could see dealing with the question, whether the right of the widow, in possession of her husband's property in lieu of her dower, to retain such possession until the same is satisfied, is transferable at all. But it is a well settled law that a person in peaceful possession of land as against everyone but the true owner, has interest capable of being conveyed. The Learned Judge also conceded that the widow can transfer the right to retain the possession of the property though along with the dower debt........" To get the true position of law on the point in issue, it is essential to distinguish between the transfer of the right to remain possession and the transfer of the property itself. Dealing with the nature of the widow's possession, it is laid down in Mohd.Ussuddolah Khan Vs. Mst.Ghashea Bebee[80] that she was temporarily in possession as a security for the payment of her dower claim. In this case the widow had alienated the property itself and it was held that the heirs could sue to avoid the transfer. The judgment runs as follows "It is clear that they (heirs) may be entitled to recover possession by payment to the debt, during her life-tine or on her death and temporarily in her possession as a security for the payment of her dower claim does not belong to them. It must be carefully noted that what the widow had alienated was not her debt with its security but the property itself, and that as to the rights of the other heirs, it is clearly laid down that they are entitled to recover possession only on payment during her life time or on her death." It was held in Mst.Kumur-ul-Nissa Begum Vs. Mahomed Hussain[81] that the widow was competent to alienate permanently more than her own one eighth share obtained by inheritance and the learned Judge remarked that "She holds it as security for the payment of her dower. At the same time, we are satisfied that the property in suit forward a portion of widow's husband's estate, the whole of which was in her possession as security for dower. The widow would have had power to mortgage such hypothecated interest, and that during her life time the widow except by payment of the dower, could not have realized the mortgage." The above analyzed two decisions of 1866 show that the widow's security for her dower is transferable, though she has not power to transfer the actual property. On the authority of these two decisions Mr. Justice Tudball observed that "The right to hold possession is one which the widow secures as a creditor for her dower and it is one to continue holding until her debt is satisfied. Such a right is property and is prima facie in the absence of any law of contract to the contrary, transferable." It may be pointed out that the earlier rulings emphasis the view that the widow in such circumstances holds the property as security for her dower-debt and acquires a lien on it and that her right to continue in such possession, is a transferable interest. This right must not be confounded with right to sell the actual property, which has been often claimed.

The Muslim widow, who is in possession of her husbands estate, is entitled to retain possession, until her dower-debt is satisfied, is competent to transfer that right, is pin-point on which there are several decisions of various courts. That the courts while considering the transferability of the right differ on the question, whether such a right is transferable without transferring the dower debt necessarily along with it? One set of pronouncements support the view that the right to hold possession cannot be served from the dower-debt and cannot be transferred as a separate interest. The other view, i.e. it can be transferred, is also supported by judicial pronouncements. Thus both aspects are to be examined. The Madras High Court is of the view that the right to hold possessions transferable without transferring the dower debt. There is passage in the judgment of Mr.Justice Abdur Rahim which gives a misconceived notion. The passage is thus "She, however, could transfer her right of possession along with the dower debt and the alienation must be upheld to that extent." The minute study of the whole judgment leaves no room for doubt, that in the opinion of the Learned Judge, the assignment of the dower-debt is an incident to the assignment of security itself. A Muslim widow, in possession of property belonging to her deceased husband in lieu of dower, can sell it without necessarily selling her right to receive dower. The earliest decision of the Patna High Court on this point is Nabijan Vs. Sahifan[82] There Mr. Justice Das and Mr. Justice Coutts dealt with the matter briefly being apparently under the impression that the Privy Council had already considered it in Ali Baksh Vs. Allahbad Khan[83], where Mr. Justice Tudball observed that: "Such right is property and is prima facie in the absence of any law of contract to the contrary, transferable." It can be pointed out that it was a decision not of the judicial committee of the Privy Council but of a

Divisional Bench of the Allahabad High Court consisting of Mr. Justice Richards and Justice Tudball very shortly after the case of Nabijan Vs. Sahifan[84] was decided the point, again came before the same Division Bench in Bibi Makbul-un-Nissa Vs. Bibi Umat-un-Nisa[85] Mr. Justice Das went into the point at much greater length and expressed the opinion that :"Where a Muslim widow in possession of her husband's property in lieu of dower transfers the security, either with or without dower-debt, the transfer is entitled to retain the possession of the property until the dower-debt is paid, though where the transfer is without the priority of the persons bound to discharge the dower debt, the transferee takes the security subject to the state of account between the widow and the persons bound to discharge the dower debt at the date of the transfer and any payment made by these persons to the widow after, but without notice, the transfer must in he absence of collusion be allowed to these persons as against the transferee. This is a view of equity which is of general application and there is no reason why we should not apply the principle in a case of transfer of security by a Muslim widow holding possession of her husband's estate as a security for the dower-debt due to her." The view taken in the above referred case is correct and approach is right. The property in possession of the widow is clearly transferable in law and the transferee of such a property from the widow would acquire a valid title so long as the debt is not satisfied. The interest which the widow had, to retain possession of the property, would pass to the transferee and there seems no reason in law or equity, why such transfer itself, should not be held valid apart from the dower debt. As back as 1927, again another Division Bench of the Patna High Court consisting of Mr. Justice Das and Mr. Justice Kulwant Sahay considered the same question in Mst. Sogia Vs. Mst. Kitaban.[86] Mr. Justice Kulwant Sahay held that a widow in possession of her husband's property in lieu of dower-debt can transfer the security apart from the dower debt and the transferee acquires a valid little so long as the debt is not satisfied. In this case what was transferred under the deed of gift by the widow was the security and not the dower debt. After reviewing the case it is candid enough that the case is different where there is a self of the property and not an assignment of the security. The distinction has not been kept in view in the various cases, which have been decided on the point but the distinction is an important one and it can not be ignored. The right to hold property as a security for the dower debt and to continue in possession thereof until the debt is a satisfied is property and is transferable. But the widow has no proprietary title in the property except to the extent of her share therein, and where she purports to sell the property and not the security only, the sale is utterly inefficient, so as to confer no title on the vendee. It is pointed out that the actual position of law according to these decisions, therefore, is this that where a Muslim widow in possession of her husband's property as a security for her dower debt, purports to sell the property and puts the vendee in possession of the property, the vendee is entitled to retain possession of the property, so long as her claim to the dower remains unsatisfied, the heirs cannot claim to be put in possession of the property and the widow herself would be bound to make good her representation to the vendee to the extent of such interest as she could lawfully transfer. There is nothing to prevent her from putting some one else in possession of the property and conferring on him the same right which she could exercise over the property herself. Having done so, the vendee will be entitled to maintain his possession as against the widow and the persons claiming through her, so long as there is a debt due to the widow. But the dower is satisfied either by payment to the widow or to her heirs, the heirs of the husband are entitled to recover possession of the property from the transferees and the same result follows where the heirs of the widow happen to be heirs of her husband, for in such an event, the right to receive the dower-debt and the liability to pay the dower debt, unite in the same person and there is extinction, both of debt and the security and therefore, of the right to retain possession of the property as a security for the debt. The Allahabad High Court expressed the view in Bindeshri Pershad Vs. Afzal Khan[87] that when the dower-debt is not transferred either expressly or impliedly alongwith the property, the widow's right of retention becomes extinguished and she cannot subsequently transfer it. The Patna High Court faced a question on this point that even if the dower was not in fact transferred, whether the widow had a lien or charge upon the property as security for enforcement of the debt, which she could transfer Dawson Miller, C.J., observed that "It was not possible for the widow to transfer the lien on the property, so as to be binding, without also transferring the dower debt. The lien on the property which gives the widow the right to retain possession until the debt has been discharged; is not an interest in the property which can be severed from the right to dower and transferred as a separate interest. It is not an interest in property, which is capable of absolute transfer."

Mr. Justice Mullick who delivered a concurring judgment relied upon the decision of the Allahabad High Court's[88] view which was later affirmed by the Privy Council's[89] the Learned Judge "The widow has a right to transfer the debt coupled with the security and that transfer will be binding upon her co-heirs, till they discharged the debt." Mr. Justice Niamatullah sharing the same view observed that "A widow could transfer her right to possession, if she also assigned her right to receive the unpaid dower. There is no valid reason in law, why she should not be entitled her debt together with her right to continue in possession. If the right to receive the dower and the right to remain in possession are vested in the same person, he cannot be ousted by the heir of the husband. If, however, the widow transfers her right to the possession of the property itself, without transferring her right to receive dower, the transferred cannot defend her right to possession as against her heirs. The ownership being vested in the heirs of the husband, the only person who can stand between him and what belongs to him is the person who is entitled to dower and to possession of the property in lieu thereof."

The conflict is with regard to the distinctions of the two rights: the right to hold possession and the right to the dower debt. Some cases have treated these rights separately, while other have mixed up the two rights. The foregoing discussion also makes it clear that the right to retain possession of husband's property, by a widow is transferable only for the widow's life. The leading case on the point is Sheikh Abdur Rahman Vs. Sheikh Wali Mohammad[90]. It was contended in this case that even if the dower debt was not in fact transferred, the widow had a lien or chare upon the property as a security for the enforcement of the debt, which she could transfer not only during her life time but even so as to ensure for the benefit of the transferee after her death. In this case, the widow was in possession in lieu of dower of the estate left by her husband which was small, the amount of unpaid dower being Rs. 4,000/-.She transferred the whole of the interest in the estate, in which she was entitled by inheritance to 'Four Annas' share to which she could undoubtedly transfer. After construing the document, Sir Dawson Miller, C.J. held that as there was not a word, from first to last, relating to any transfer of her dower-debt, he was unable to construe the document as purporting to transfer the dower debt and then observed that "Nor in my opinion, was it possible for her to transfer the lien on the property so as to be binding after her life-time, without transferring also the dower-debt. The lien on the property which gives the widow the right to possession until the debt has been discharged is not an interest in the property which can be severed from the right to dower and transferred as a separate interest. It is a right to the possession of the property by the person entitled to be paid the dower as long as the dower debt is not discharged either by the income from the property or by payment by the heirs or other interest in discharging the debt. It certainly gives the widow the right to possession and it may be assumed that as long as she does not transfer her dower-debt and that debt remains undischarged, she may transfer or her life-time possession of the property, the proceeds of which belong to her until the debt is paid off." As regards the possession of the transferee, the Learned Judge remarked that "The possession of the transferee in such a case might be regard as constructively her possession. Just as she could dispose of the proceeds in any way she choose her life time and until the debt was discharged, so also she could transfer possession of the property in same circumstances, the transferee being entitled to usufruct, but if she dies and her estate devolves upon her heirs or assignees the transferee's right to possession would be extinguished as the debt and security cannot be served thereby converting the security into a separate interest in the property. It would appear, therefore, the possession of the property, forming the security for the debt, this would not ensure to the benefit of the transferee after the widow's death, when the dower-debt passed to her heirs." In his separate concurring judgment Mr. Justice Mullick observed that "The widow may during her life-time transfer the right of possession apart from the debt but this is a matter between herself and her transferee and the transfer will not be binding upon her co-heirs after her death."

The analyses of aforesaid judicial pronouncements lead to the following propositions: -

1. That the mere transfer of the dower does not pass to the transferee the right to hold and retain possession of property.
2. That the right to hold and retain possession of the property can validly be transferred if the right to receive the unpaid dower is also transferred. If the right to receive the dower and the right to

remain in possession are transferred together, the transferee cannot be ousted by the heirs of the husband until the dower is paid off, and

3. That the right to retain possession if transferred, will remain valid and operative only during the life-time of the widow."

The right to hold and retain of deceased husband's property is considered as a personal right and is therefore incapable of alienation. In an earlier case of Mujaffar Ali Vs. Parbati[91] Allahabad High Court such right was held to be inalienable. The Learned Judge observed that "The utmost right assigned to the widow is that of a creditor to hold certain property, until her debt is satisfied such a right could never be transferable. It is nothing more than an interest in the property, restricted in its enjoyment to the owner personally and transfer of any such right is prohibited by Section 6 (d) of the Transfer of Property Act." It can be pointed out that in the first place the widow in this case was not and never had been in possession of the estate in question. That had remained all along with mortgagees, to whom the husband had given possession. It was therefore, hardly necessary for the purposes of the cases, to decide the question of the nature of the possession of a Muslim widow, lawfully obtained in lieu of dower. Secondly, no grounds are given for holding that the enjoyment of this right to continue in possession is restricted to the widow personally. The right is one" which the widow secures as a creditor for her dower and it is one to continue holding until her dower- debt is satisfied. However, their Lordships of the Privy Council[92] have expressed the doubt, whether a widow can transfer either the dower debt or the right of retention. Lord Atkinson observed to this effect that "It was contended, that Maina Bibi had by the deed of 1907 aligned both her husband's estate until that debt was paid. It is doubtful whether she could have done either of these things and she in fact, never purported or attempted to do either of them. On the contrary, in those deeds she descries herself as the absolute owner of the property of her deceased husband, purports to convey that absolute ownership to her done. There is no ground for the contention, if it has been really put forward, that because the deeds fail to affect a transfer of the absolute interest with which they purport to deal, they operate to transfer the widow's dower debt and her right to hold possession of the lands till that debt is paid. By giving up of the lands, as in her deeds she alleges she has done, she has undoubtedly lost her right to hold the possession of them." This view of their Lordships of the Privy Council was later on adopted in many cases. The Patna High Court[93] held that the dower debt of a Muslim widow is not properly speaking a charge upon the property of her husband, and the interest which she has in the property in her possession lieu of dower debt is, therefore, an interest restricted in its enjoyment to her personally within the meaning of Section 6 (d) of the Transfer of Property Act and such is not capable of alienation, whether or without the dower-debt. In a later case of the same court in Abdul Samad Vs. Alimuddin[94] a Division Bench consisting of Mr. Justice Reuban and Mr. Justice Verma reiterated the view that the right of a Muslim widow to remain in possession of her husband's property until the satisfaction of her dower debt, was a right restricted to her personally and was not capable of alienation, whether with or without the dower-debt. In this case, the widow was in possession of the one-third share in a house. She, however, transferred the whole and entire one-third share in the house which had been and was in her possession and occupation as absolute proprietor in lieu of dower debt. It was held that in these circumstances by the Learned Judges hat what the widow could transfer by sale-deed was only her one-twelfth share and that she could not transfer her right to possession of property in lieu of her dower-debt. In this case, Mr. Justice Reuban expressed the view that the matter has been set at rest by the decision of the Judicial Committee[95] and that the decision of the Patna High Court[96] was no longer good law. Reference was made in the course of arguments to the decisions of a Full Bench of the Madras High Court;[97] which expressed the contrary view. But it was held that the precedence must be given to the decision of the Privy Council and the view expressed by the Madras High Court cannot be held to be authoritative in view of the decision of the Privy Council. The same view was later on adopted in another case.[98] All these decision show that estate or interest in the property belongs all the time to the real owners. The widow has a mere right of possession that remains with her so long as she is in possession and by giving up possession; she loses her right to hold possession of them.

The study of judicial trend reveals that there is a difference of opinion between the Benches which decided the different cases as to the power of a Muslim widow in possession of her husband's property in lieu of her dower debt to transfer the security, whether with or without the dower debt and as to the effect of a transfer by the widow of her entire interest in the property, without transferring her dower debt upon her right to remain in possession of the property in lieu of her dower debt. There is a balance of authority in favour of the view that the widow's right to retain possession of her husband's estate in lieu of her dower debt is transferable along with the right to dower or without it. But this cannot be regarded as settled law in view of the fact that their Lordships of the Privy Council have expressed the doubt as to whether the widow can assign either her dower debt or the right to hold possession of her husband's estate until the payment of the debt. In some cases, it was observed that the decision of the Privy Council has shaken the authority of the earlier decisions of the Patna High Court. But the Mysore High Court, after the decision of the Privy Council has held that a widow of a Muslim who is lawfully in possession of her husband's estate can retain such possession until her dower debt is satisfied. That right may be transferred along with her share provided the same is done by proper and valid deed of conveyance. The transfer must include the right to remain in possession and the transferee must also be put in possession. If the widow or her transferee is out of possession, they can not sue for possession on the basis of the right retain possession.

Thus the judicial analysis on the point clarifies that the conflict still exists. This conflict can not be resolved only by the Supreme Court of India either by coming to the rescue of the transferee of the widow or by coming to the rescues of the heirs of the husband, however, on the basis of real purpose of the case-law following conclusion can be drawn In some cases,[99] it has been held that the right of retention is not transferable at all and the other hand of judicial opinion establishes that the right of retention which a Muslim widow secures as a creditor in lieu of dower-debt becomes property right and is prima facie transferable.[100] The balance of authority supporter the view that it is transferable right, but the Privy Council decision[101] has caused some ambiguity whether the widow can assign her personal right or right to retention although the matter was not decided to its finality.

The other judicial opinion available supports that although the right of retention in lieu of unpaid dower is transferable, yet it can be transferred only along with the dower-debt and not separately. Contrary to it judicial opinion is there which supports that widow can transfer her right of retention without parting with her dower debt. One question yet to be judicially satisfied: assume, the right of retention in lieu of dowerdebt is transferable instead of transferring her lien, the widow transfer the property and deliver possession to transferee, in such circumstance will the transfer be assumed to be valid in respect of the retention right or will the transferee be entitled to keep possession? On this issue in some cases it has been deduced that the transfer will operate on valid footing in respect of right of lien. Contrary to it the judicial opinion in series of cases establishes that if widow transfers the property retained in lieu of unpaid dower without expressly or impliedly transferring the lien, the right of, retention will stand extinguished.

Conclusively speaking, the position of transferee of the right of retention from the widow is still uncertain.

Mortgage and the Right of Retention

The position of a widow claiming to retain possession of her husband's property until her dower debt it paid, is essentially different from that of a mortgage (usufructuary or other) to whom the: owner pledges his property to secure repayment of a debt. The interest of the widow in the property of her deceased husband is not that of a mortgagee, as there is no real true analogy at all between her right of retention and a mortgage usufructuary or otherwise. Judiciary has amply made clear through the Privy Council in Maina Bibi Vs. Vakil Ahmad[102]. It was contended that the position of a widow in possession of her husband's estate was analogous to that of a mortgagee in possession. But this contention was not accepted by their Lordships and Lord Atkinson observed that "In the case of a mortgage the mortgagee takes and retains possession under an agreement or arrangement made between him and the mortgagor. But in case of widow's right of retention neither the possession of the property nor the right to retain the possession of the property when acquired is conferred upon the widow by the agreement or bounty of her deceased husband. The possession of the property, the right of the widow to retain it till her dower debt is paid, is conferred by Mohammedan Law. The husband, when he grants dower to his wife cannot by any original hypothecation of his property, secure to her the payment of it. But the original and intentional hypothecation of the mortgaged property to secure the payment of the mortgage debt is the very essence of every mortgage, usufructuary or other. The widow who

Printed by BoD™ in Norderstedt, Germany

9 781805 251705